This book is to be returned on or before the last date stamped below.

CHILDREN AS POETS

CHILDREN AS POETS

Edited, with a Postscript,
by
Denys Thompson

HEB

HEINEMANN
LONDON

Heinemann Educational Books Ltd
LONDON EDINBURGH MELBOURNE TORONTO
AUCKLAND JOHANNESBURG SINGAPORE
IBADAN NAIROBI HONG KONG NEW DELHI

ISBN 0 435 14893 1

821
THO

Published by
Heinemann Educational Books Ltd
48 Charles Street, London W1X 8AH

Set in Monotype Plantin

Printed in Great Britain by
Butler & Tanner Ltd, Frome and London

Contents

List of Illustrations

Foreword

This collection of poems by writers of five to about eighteen has been made for the enjoyment of the general reader. Children's art, drama and music-making receive their fair share of attention, but for lack of a substantial anthology of verse by young people the quality of their writing is less generally known. This book aims at filling the gap, and at illustrating the high standard of their work; the poetry they produce represents a more solid achievement and one of stronger appeal to adults than that of their other artistic endeavours, simply because the language that is so much a part of being human is more developed, more immediately at their disposal and more effective at communicating than other modes of expression.

Moreover, because language is so integral with their being, the writing of poetry meets an immediate need of young people, as a means of moral and emotional growth—to say nothing of improvement in the art of writing. It is for this reason that teachers encourage the writing of free verse among their pupils—a practice that is totally different from courses in 'creative writing'. This educational aspect is considered at greater length in the Postscript (p. 171), so called and placed because the poems need no explanation or apology, and ask for no allowances to be made. They are not the apprentice work of adult poets, for few will write verse after leaving school; but they are always interesting and often engaging, in the recurrent freshness of perception that appears in many of the writers and in the courageous and movingly human response of others to scenes and situations. The poems are much more rewarding than the general run of verse published nowadays.

D. T.

Family

[1]

I hav for breakfast Weetabix
I hav for lunch some meat
I have for tea 2 sosajis
   and thats enuf to eat

                 Peter Hazel, 5

[2]

My Brother

My brother is a little —?—.
He has done everything there is to do,
And the thing is I get the blame.
He's crafty, he's a little horror,
And the thing is that he's brainy.
He sits and thinks
Sits and thinks
Thinks of pranks he can pull on me.
The little horror him.
Why can't little boys emigrate?

                 Gary Marsh, 15

[3]

My Sister

My little sister, who is five years old,
Spends her life making mine a misery.
According to Mum she does everything she's told,
But not where I am concerned,
For I must not take her things, she is not supposed
  to take mine.
Although she does.

3

I argue and say I want them back.
'Oh no,' says mum, 'you should not fight;
After all, Nicola is only five and you are
    thirteen.'
I make the beds and do the washing-up,
I go to the shops but I don't get any thanks,
'Mind the wet floor, hang up your coat,'
It wasn't like this before Nicola came.

Christine Suckling, 13

[4]

Teach Him a Lesson

A parent having an afternoon rest suddenly
Hears a crash.
Woken from his sleep and cross
He strides up the stairs
To find, upon the floor,
A broken toy.
The child sits
With thunder on his face, which changes
To fear as his father stamps in.
He struggles and shouts in his father's arms
As he's shaken and walloped
To teach him a lesson.
The father gets more cross, the child
More defiant, and he goes on
Beating him as a punishment, then, exhausted,
He lets go of the child,
Who is breathlessly told
Not to do it again.
The child promises faithfully, but,
As soon as his father's gone,
He jumps again on the toy, to break it
Into hundreds of pieces.
His father returns, and, his temper lost,
He hits him and sends him to bed for the rest of the day.

Graham Paddon

[5]

Memories

I remember my first enemy.
The pert, provoking child they said was my cousin.
I remember despising her straight limp hair,
The green glowering eyes,
And her slight, lively body.
And that she despised my fluffy brown curls,
Pink complexion,
And plumpness.
They made us learn to dance together.
She was clumsy,
Her mouth pouted when she danced
But she said I was too fat to dance.
I wasn't.
They made us walk to school together.
She didn't even know her tables.
She couldn't knit.
I could knit when I was five,
But she laughed at me.
At home they made us play together:
She prodded me with bony fingers,
She pushed me down the stairs.
And when I saw her laughing
I screamed, until she cried.
I remember how I hated my cousin.

Rosalind Levi, 14

[6]

Mother

Grey haired she sits
Watching
Bemused by the Saint
Entranced by Humperdinck
Enthralled by Peyton Place

Yet disgusted at
'The Wednesday Play'
And missing the point
Of 'At the Eleventh Hour'.

Grey haired she sits
Eyes flashing
Lecturing me on
The virtues of hard work
And keeping up appearances
(For the neighbours
So they can see
I'm not a yob).

Grey haired she lies
Arms crossed on her breast
In traditional reverence.
In my imagination
She lies in
Peaceful hold of death.
And yet I wonder
Will I weep
Or dance on her grave?

Nick Dellar, 15

[7]

Parents

They tell you what to do each day and night,
But, yet, I suppose, they mean us well.
Kind, ever considerate, ever watchful,
We're forever at the difficult age,
But, still, we would be hopeless without them.

One is masterful, sometimes too much,
Whereas the female is fussy and vain,
Proud and pompous, like mother hens

They sit watching our every move,
Chastising, encouraging;
Seeing their wildest dreams fulfilled,
Or disappointed in our failure,
Encouraging us to try again.
Providing us with our lives and health,
No wonder they want to keep us here.

Moira Driscoll, 15

[8]

Mother

At night when all was quiet
    and the moon was still,
My mother's mind raced back,
    back many years,
Back to the days she wore
    those dresses she adored.
Then she moved towards the piano,
    her fingers slid across the key-board,
The soft mellow music made its way
    through the old boards of the house to my room.
I longed to embrace her, but I wanted her
    to keep her dream.
As the night went on my mother
    played to the tune of her memories,
 The days she wore those dresses
    now many years out of style.
She played on, on through her daze,
    the daze of her past life,
A daze she wished she was
    living in
And she lived it every night,
    every night of her life
Till the end.

Robert Murphy, 14

[9]

Fishing

Every Sunday my dad goes fishing.
And we all at home have to clean upstairs
And downstairs
While my dad is fishing
We at home are all slaving away to clean up.
And when my dad came home
He had the cheek to say
Go and do your Mam's bedroom.
So I said
You go fishing all morning
Expecting to have your dinner on the table.
Then you go to hospital
And come home to sleep
Until your tea is ready.
So you can go and do Mam's bedroom.
I had to go and do Mam's bedroom.
But all the same I told him
What I thought about him going fishing
And then telling us to do this and that.

Denise Nicholls, 13

[10]

When Dad's gone out

O! it's so lonely when Mother's not in,
There's pears on the dish
There's sweets in the tin;
But there's no fun when Mother's not in.

O, what fun when Dad's gone out,
Mother and I can laugh and shout,
We have a big fire in the grate
And Dad's not there to make a complaint.

Veronica

The Second Child

The mother was contented,
Her second baby coming.
She wondered what it would be:
A boy or girl—'or even a fairy' she tittered.

The first child was a boy,
He was three.
He didn't know of the brain, or 'deficiency'.
He was innocent, but knew he had a brother or
    sister coming.

At last; nine months passed.
The mother went to hospital.
The father went a few hours later,
The boy stayed with the nurse at home.

The sister came out quietly,
She said, 'Come this way, sir,
I must tell you something'. He was astonished—
'Not usual', he muttered, but followed meekly.

He was alone now, in the office.
Security and home, no more:
The baby, a mongol—how awful.
He nearly died.

For some time the mother wasn't seen
By the boy or the nurse, the father knew
And gradually calmed himself.
Two weeks later she returned.

A week after that the baby came.
Mother and father and the boy,
With the nurse, awaited it. Father
Felt green. The boy delighted with a sister.

Nurse knew the boy would not realise
For two years or more. Father picked up babe—
She felt normal, looked fairly normal,
But wasn't.

After six months, mother was contented,
Boy was happy, and nurse worked.
Father, feeling only blue, would pick her up,
She didn't speak, only smiled.

At a year, the difference was marked:
She couldn't speak—wouldn't;
But could play a little—like a puppy.
Father played too.

He, now, was better—his work as good as ever;
His boss was pleased, and vaguely sympathetic
At the right moments. He could play with, to her,
By her. He almost loved her.

At last, boy was seven. He must know!
She was four now. On every other day she went
To a special school. She loved them in almost
A feline way, he knew.

Boy looked at her for some time
And loved her still. One day,
At Easter Time, they all went
To a photographer, to pose.

They posed. They smiled—they loved;
The picture is now in the sitting room,
In Dad's wallet, on Mother's table,
In boy's room. The picture is held by her

As a charm; she's there, one of them, at home.
Loved.

M. Macgregor, 15

Uncle Died

Uncle is dead.

Johnny and I remember,
when we were younger and lived over the shop,
the Sunday rides.

The mumbles, stumbles,
cough and spit.
The tight muffler, the Woodbines that made
the phlegm-sea tickle and splash.

But we moved.
Uncle became a fat obstacle,
parked in the largest armchair,
slippered, immune from sense and sensation,
gravy-stains on his waistcoat, fag-ash.
A burbling semi-domesticated animal,
another piece of furniture.

Sometimes he would wake and gibber Yiddish
till we called Dad
and he would tell Uncle that he must
speak English so that the kids could understand.

Uncle shrugged—and went back to sleep.

Uncle is dead,
there's no gap, no aching hole,
nothing.

Dad says we're all a bloody sight better off.
Is Uncle?
He could only be partly conscious of his own existence,
Sleeping when he was awake.
He never laughed at the T.V.
It was in English.

Dan, 15

[13]

Grandparents

Old and gnarled; wizened faces dreaming of
Past days gone by.
Living in their own world:
Christmasses; presents;
Easter; church service on television;
Telling of experiences, adding bits here and there
To improve the story;
Surprised at the cost of living; not understanding
Why prices go up and up;
Enjoying company, but company not enjoying
Them. Yet happy in their own way.

Sheila Bramfit

[14]

Night Scene

Maybe it's fate or just coincidental
But an argument always starts at night.
And in the confusion of tempers and anger
It's on with the coat, a blatant slam of the door
And outside into the night.

The night's such a soothing time
For as you walk swiftly, away from the trouble,
The darkness, the stillness, the quietness, even the coldness,
Slows you down
And, head bowed, you creep along the uneven pavement,
Watching your feet continuously stepping in front of one
    another.
Trying to concentrate.
But you can't
For there is so much and yet so little happening around you,
That all distracts you.

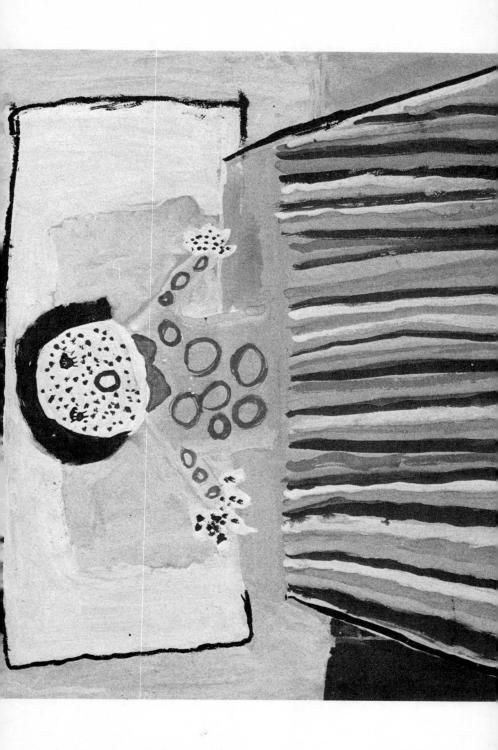

How dark it all is,
How beautiful the gleaming stars are set in a
Background of nothing.
How cold they look,
How cold it is.
So cold you can see your breath diminishing in silence.
How silent.
How softly the old street lamps throw a soothing
Lightness onto the dark pavements.

But such beauty aids thought.
Thought aids remembrance.
How vile the closed coloured curtains are
When the house-lights are burning.
How ridiculous the over-volumed televisions sound.

How maddening the laughter from within four walls gets,
Why do they laugh and mock
The very beauty of the darkness, the stillness,
The quietness.
Who are they to spoil it all?
Why is it that those who suffer, suffer alone?

Time passes by,
The cold becomes unbearable,
And after walking round in one big circle,
You return, unspeaking, to the trouble you left.
But in the morning all is forgiven and forgotten.

                                                S. Farnall, 16

[15]

My Last Look

I walked down the path slowly,
I looked back,
Tears filled my eyes when I saw
My small brother staring at me through the window.
My mother and father were standing at the door

With my baby sister.
I had never seen them look so sad before,
Nor had I felt so sad.
I stared back at the house,
Wanting to run back to it,
I walked a few more steps.
My dog barked
And father held him back when he tried to run to me.
I wanted to run back, but
Something was stopping me.
What would my brother say when I did not return?
What would my mother and father talk about when I had gone?
What would I do without my dog?
Where would I go?
What would I do?
These questions went over and over in my mind
As I walked.
My tears blinded me.
I wiped them away and turned round to see my family for the
    last time.

Anne Colquitt, 15

Town

A Foggy Road

The murky, clammy, sinister looking fog,
Swirls dismally round,
Enveloping the cumbersome, blundering tanker.
The muffled throb of the diesel engine,
Comes faintly through the fog.
The tanker ploughs on.
In the isolated cab,
The driver smells the acrid stench of fuel.
A scooter zips through the eerie fog,
The beam from its fog lamp probing the haze.
The frozen rider heaves a sigh of relief

As he comes out of the monotony of the fog,
Into the pool of light round a solitary street lamp.
Ahead, the tanker's exhaust belches out black smoke,
Making the fog even thicker
The two vehicles move on.
Through the murk of the fog.

D. L. Whittingham, 11

The Song of the Dustbin

Wrap it up in papery wapery
All the junk and dapery lapery,
Get rid of all the wasty gapery
Dirty, donty, dooth.
Clankily clonkily goes the donkery
Inkery bankery went the ronkily,
Taking out of all the rubbishly
Slimey, slonky, slooth.
Thinkery thonkery thought the thunkily
Slithy slothy went the lunkily,
Crashing all the zinkily zunkily
Mingle, mangle, mooth.

Here's the dustman thompy thumpery
Come to get the bins for umpery,
Carry them on their backsy bumpery
Jogery, jamily, jooth.
Put it in the lorryly loomily
Start it up quonkily quoomily,
Down the road screechy scroomily
Finkily, fonkily, footh.
Turn the corner sharpily soothily
Now we're at the dumpy doothily,
Empty it on the rest of the mungily
Kunkily, konkery, kooth.
There it lies for many a century
Going all bad and rotting rentury,
Twenty yards and pooey pongery

Camily, comily, cooth.
Here's a bulldozer faloomfily flomithily
Come to now the dumpy doothily,
Never again to nothily noothily
This is the song of the dustbin.

Michael Scott, 14

[18]

Condemned

The school stands inconspicuous in the snow,
Forbidding, yet pleading to be used.
Memories of the past hang in the corridors.
Rotting doors creak sorrowfully.
Desks, engraved with names
Of those long dead, are stacked in the corner.
As if trying to hide the past,
And look towards the future.
But what future has it?
The demolition crews are moving in.

Marilyn Brown, 15

[19]

Snow or Work?

He sits alone,
Sighing over his homework,
Outside in the snow,
And everything looks perfect;
The pavement is no longer cracked,
And the litter has gone.
There is only a gentle white lake
To be seen.
Its surface is slightly rippled.
He sees his friends playing outside,
But he can't join in.
He must do his homework.
A snowball hits the window;
He would like to throw one back,
But he can't.
Yet he sees his arch-enemy,
And he thinks only of revenge
For the last time they met.
So he leaves his work,
Puts his coat and gloves on,
And rushes out.
After squeezing two snowballs
He begins to stalk his prey.
A few more steps . . .
'Adrian, come and finish your work.'
He slowly walks back to the house,
His feet sag in the whiteness.
In front of him is a cracked snowball:
He kicks it into the emptiness.

S. M. Lam, 13

[20]

Supermarket

The smell was wrong:
Not a savoury 'Sainsbury' smell,
But a perfumed hypocrisy.

The meat,
Carefully lit for maximum colour,
Odourless and tasteless,
Blood-red
In a deodorised refrigerator.
Lulling soothing music
Insidiously hypnotising,
And a cash-desk queue
Four minutes long—
But stamps at the end.

John Lees

[21]

A Poem about a Statue

He stands there still, cold and grey,
His arm held in one position
By cold, grey stone,
His cloak carved out of solid rock,
His face sad and forlorn
Standing in sadness,
For being a captive clapped in stone.

I look at him and wonder
How his limbs must ache
Standing in the same position
For all the centuries he has endured,
Through tornado and storm,
Siege and war.

Andrew Mudd, 11

[22]

Leather Jackets, Bikes and Birds

The streets are noisy
with the movement of passing motors.
The coffee bar gets fuller.

The leather-jacket groups begin to gather,
stand, and listen, pretending they are
looking for trouble.
The juke box plays its continuous
tune, music appreciated by Most.
The aroma of Espresso
coffee fills the nostrils and
the night.
Motor bikes pull up.
Riders dismount and join
their friends in the gang.
They stand, smoking, swearing,
playing with the girls;
making a teenage row.
They pretend not to notice the drizzle,
falling out of the dark,
because you've got to be hard to
be a leather-jacket.
A couple
in a corner, snogging,
hope the motor lights will not be
dipped too much,
so that the others will see them.
They must all have recognition;
there must always be enough
leather jackets around them,
the same as theirs.
The street lamp on the side
of the street shows the rain
for what it is—wet and cold.
But it does not show their faces
for what they are.

Boy, 16

[23]

Trawlerman's Son

Docks, sleeping and deserted.
White bollards, chipped and rusting,
Stand on the damp and oily quayside.

Chains lie like bronze snakes
Rusting on the ground.
Warehouses hungry for goods wait
Starving in the shadows, and lorries wait
Dormant and empty.
Seagulls creak overhead, bringing news
No-one will understand.
Oil slaps, laps,
Against the quay. No foghorns sound now.
The smell of diesel fuel, oil and seaweed
Pervades one's nostrils. But all
The docks know is silence, and
A boy nearly dead with waiting.

Andrew Foster, 16

[24]

The Trawler

The dense smoke hung around the lamps,
Flavouring the air with the tang of oil,
As the trawler, silhouetted against the moon,
Churned the greys and the greens into white screwthreads,
Which rose to the surface
In bubbles and were enveloped by the heaving sea.

The winches strained at the greased cables,
And oil-skinned sailors stood amid the white spray
Preparing to grab the net.
Suddenly it emerged from the sea
And was swung, dripping, over the deck.
Orders were shouted and obeyed:
And the net emptied its load of fat and wriggling fish.

L. Turner, 17

[25]

The Metal Monsters

Here is a meadow sleeping peacefully under the sun;
Corn waves softly, grasses whispering to each other,
And then from the north the metal monsters come.

And boots take the place of daisy roots,
Bulldozers bashing, cranes crashing,
Tractors tearing, dumpers mashing,
Loaded lorries lumbering, bouncing, hanging.
Listen to the roaring, snorting, growling,
   screaming, screeching of the metal monsters,
And then the monsters go away,
And down comes the snow as the monsters go away.
And there stands the house tall and grey.

Ewan Beattie, 12

[26]

Life

The plain marsh
The plain motorway
Those huge stretches of green land
The hiring of man
The hugeness and incredible vastness
And the ugliness
They came with tractors
Sanded and large
To blow up the greenland.

They broke the fences
Cleaned the country of the living
And brought concrete.

G. R. Mitchell, 16

[27]

Wasteland

Rainbow coloured water and rank grass.
Stretched for as far as one could see.
The great chimney of the brickworks
Dominated the hills.

Dirty black smoke puffed out,
Discolouring the sky.
The waters, river bed and vegetation,
Were rimmed and coated with emerald smelly slime.

Rusty iron and steel frames,
Tin cans and broken chairs and beer bottles.
Engulfed the marshland.
Here mans refuse had taken over.

Mark Chaplin, 10

[28]

Bingo!

Sitting, waiting.
The score-cards grasped in grimy sweating hands.
Grasped as tightly as a life-line,
The thread leading through the maze of life to wealth,
The massed greed rises like the cigarette smoke.
The caller on the stage, his eyes hard,
Laughing at the inanities which roll out
     monotonously.
Tension reigns, not excitement.
People twist nervously in their seats,
Surreptitiously wiping their hands on their coats
Waiting, waiting.
Crossing off their numbers one by one
Like the ticking from a clock.
Time runs out. The alarm goes off.
A thin, cracked voice from the balcony shrieks
     'Full House' again and again
As if each repetition was an incantation to
     secure full payment.
A sharply indrawn breath from the crowd.
A rustle of craning necks then a collective sigh.
They get up and go to their homes.

N. G. Jeffs, 17

Envisaged by man;
Conceived by the Industrial Revolution;
Consisting of a sprawling, monochromatic desert
   of serried semis;
Created by man.
Reluctantly inhabited by man;
He alleviates the monotony with
Gaudy hoardings,
Overhead transmission lines,
Red pillar boxes.
Yesterday's green belts,
Today's housing redevelopment,
Tomorrow's slum clearance.
Target of the advertising manager,
Home of the average man;
Birth place of many,
Cemetery for thousands.
Triangulated by town halls;
Stimulated by the Electricity Board;
Motivated by rates and taxes.
A collection of constituencies.
A labyrinth of Terraces, Avenues and Roads,
Crescents, Walks and Groves,
Rows, Lanes and Streets;
A copper's beat,
A postman's nightmare;
A veritable subtopia.
Restless dormitory of the metropolis:
The necessary evil, but not sufficient in itself—
Despised by man.

Boy, 17

Domestic Nature

Commons are despicable things.
Like zoos or pekinese or a budgie's clipped wings,
Or the most abhorrent botanical garden
Where they instal, quite without pardon,
Hard things like railings and bird-baths,
And stone steps and coquettish concrete paths.

But a common I detest most of all.
Its tame trees, its quaintly-rooted paths are gall
To me. With undergrowth listless, shabby,
The whole seems limp and flabby—
Like a middle-aged business-man
Whose body rots as unjust serving-man
To a conceited brain. In this false
Nature, as wild and free as a waltz
We comatose humans stroll smugly,
Murmur 'Delightful!' It should be 'Ugly!'
And where we blindly pass the boy-smooth bough,
We should reap and remember how;
For we have forgotten how to live.

                                        Boy, 18

Contemporaries

[31]

Loneliness

Let me play I beg you.
Go away we don't want you.
Oh please let me play
it's lonely with no friends
And I feel wanted.
They play nice games but I
can't play oh please.
No don't keep asking we shan't let you play
I can't play by myself.
Yes, you can you're only making things up so go and play.

When I go home I hear them saying
What shall we do tonight?
We can play cowboy and we can have my tent
Oh what can we have to sit on
we can have my mummy's old rug
So when I go home I read a book.

                                        Susan Desborough, 7

[32]

Brownies

I felt lonely and new
Why did I ever come?
Know-one forced me to
I was being stupid.

All these new faces
All in the same uniform
I was different
From the other Brownies

The children were different
Their belts slipped down

Their ties were tatty and crooked
They had different coloured shoes.

We had new games
New things to work at
New things to see
Brown Owl was new.

It was terrible
There was not a single friendly face
I thought it was ghastly
But I soon got used to it
I love it now.

Susan Mangam, 9

[33]

First Impressions

The green door swung
Out into the cold, dark, stone corridor.
I pursued the Headmaster
Into an alien land of faces
Erupting from pink and blue striped blazers
Hurriedly rising in rattling desks
And killing their conversations.
A beaming, terribly young, form-master
Directed me to my desk
And parleyed with the Headmaster,
My one human contact in this silent room
Of strange, gaping, curious inmates.
None of them exist now;
For they have changed identity and appearance,
And become
Members of *my* form.

John Lees

[34]

Jealousy

Girls in school, what do they think of each other?
Every day going around doing the same old things,
But thinking different thoughts.
Some are jealous, thinking:
Why is she better than me?
Why should she get all the praise?
And gradually a small piece of childish jealousy
Turns into a fiery hate.
Everything she does is hated, jeered at, scorned,
Like an angry volcano
Which is only quiet when she is wrong or hurt.
Jealousy, should it ever triumph over the minds of men?
Bringing hurt and sorrow to many,
Making them different from what they are.
A gentle kind person, if given the reason,
Will change
To something which is like a disease,
Hurting, bringing great sadness,
And sometimes even death.

                                   Bridget Osborne, 12

[35]

A Girl Called Betty

I know a girl called Betty,
She was waiting down my road,
For me! for me! for me!
I wonder why I said,
'I would dread
To go with her'.
I wonder why.

                            Boy, 13

[36]

Hands

Your silent hand bears more severity, more goodness
Than all your loud words ever can express.
How comforting its gentle touch can be
Where words would only hurt me,
And how wonderful are the works it creates
When your heart is full of delight.

Your hand tells more plainly your grief and compassion
Than your face's vague expression;
For your eyes and your words can deceive—
But never your hand's relief.

Beatrice Debrunner (Switzerland)

[37]

Mac

They call him Mac and make fun of him,
He is too afraid to fight back.

Mac! Mac! they yell at him and he leaves
His seat and goes to them.
They tease him and in the end they
Tease him so much that he strikes
With his fists but misses them.

They try to make him mad again.
Mac! Mac! you can't catch us Mac!
He comes to them again and
Catches a boy who he brings
Hurling to the ground.

When he gets up he goes for him
Again.
Mac! Mac! let go of me Mac.

The boy wears a tattered coat and
His unbrushed hair is blown in the
Wind.

John Williams, 14

[38]

East End Boy

Smoke surls upward past peeling wallpaper,
Windows are broken, advertisement covered,
Two chairs, one table, tilts, broken,
Like the home.

Outside the buses growl through the drifting rain,
Street lamps burn unblinking, down in the gutter paper is
    racing,
The cat struts lonely, like the boy.

Under the light he stands, long hair glossy, jeans unwashed,
Shirt clings sodden, he scrapes his thin shoes,
Couples walk by touched by love, needing love,
Like the Boy.

Can't go home, fears his father, mother is drinking (Drink
drowns the home)
Among the bins a dog is searching,
Like the Boy.

C. Priest

[39]

In the Evening

Picks and shovels put aside,
Boots are polished with skill and care,
As one by one the navvy men set out to enjoy themselves.
Six full days of working, sweat, toil and misery.

And what do you get to repay your toil?
A grubby pay packet!
But at least it's good and honest work,
And it keeps the hungry mouths of your family shut.

The contrast to the cold night air
In the small and grimy pub,
The hazy smoke, the drink and sweat,
Is alarmingly different, when you come to think.
A small boy blinks uncertainly,
His first time in a pub.
He glances at the bar-maid,
A friendly-looking woman, powdered and blushing,
At the rough-voiced compliments.

'What'll you have?' comes a boisterous voice
From a small squat man,
The landlord, a sly, bowlegged man,
A gentleman of his class, grins easily,
But the nervous lad takes to his heels
And bolts.

Girl, 13

[40]

By the Roadside

Here the roadside trees splash shade,
And the tangle of grass holds coolness still;
Hikers we rest from the long hill
By a drooping fence, and the meal is laid.

Past and away over the landscape dun
A gaggle of racing cyclists dare the sun;
Pleasant to count them; pleasanter to muse
On what they gain that we perhaps may lose.

What are they heading for, hell-for-leather?
What do they seek in the summer weather,
Dust in their faces,
Those swift light racers?

Only the macadam miles for spurning?
Only the sea, the point of their turning?
Only another bright day for the burning?

What are they seeking, hell-for-leather,
Those swift light racers, huddled together? . . .
What do we find, watching the riot
From the sheltered green of the hedge's quiet?
We find ourselves—in the quietness of gazing
Where the sun spreads a brightness beyond, and a
  shadow for lazing.

R. E. Pritchard, 18

[41]

Thugs

Flick knives, pen knives,
Studded belts and big buckles,
And anything that will cut
or bruise the human body.

Cigarette ends, glowing in the dark,
and round the alleys,
or on the corner of a street,
There is a dim silence.

Rockers, Mods,
In cafes until midnight,
On motor cycles, and scooters
As they fade away in the darkness,
And the silence is once more King.

Rockers waiting outside pubs,
Waiting to pick up some talent,
Then off on their motorbikes they go,
And sometimes never see tomorrow.

Barry Heaton, 11

Burn up along the M.1.
My life I'm doing a ton.
Way up into third
Just to thrill my bird.

Tonning it now along the M.1.
Fast as a bullet from a gun,
'Down into second.'
That's what she reckoned.

She said, 'Go slow.
I'm too young to go.'
But I was away
Speeding it up that day.

Then came that bend.
I knew it was the End.
Slipped down into first.
To last, Death had cursed.

My bike slipped from my hands,
I was thrown aside on the sands.
But my bird stayed on and hit the wall
To this very day I can hear her call.

[43]

Ballad of the Teddyboy

The wind was a torrent of darkness, running an endless race;
The moon was a silvery rocket, careering through outer space;
The road was bathed in neon, a pageant for man to anoint;
Then the Teddyboy came riding to Charlie's Hamburger Joint.

Chorus:

Up to the car seat he vaulted. He jiggled the keys on the dash.
Coughing, the engine turned over and Wham! he was off in
a flash.

He'd a Donovan cap on his forehead, acne all over his chin,
A jacket of smooth black leather; dungarees neat as a pin
Except for a few random grease spots; his engineer boots reached
  his thigh.
His knuckleduster a twinkle under the jewelled sky.

Chorus: As before.

He kicked up the dust in the driveway as his brakes cut the air
  like a knife;
He revved his engine a few times to call for the love of his life.
He leaned on his horn for a minute, and who should come from
  the back
But Shirley, the owner's daughter, munching a hamburger snack.

Chorus: as before.

'How 'bout a kiss, huh, Shirley? I've done a job tonight,
And I'm back with a roll of bills but he put up quite a fight.
He wouldn't hand it over, so I used me wrench on his head,
And the cops are after me see,' the bold daredevil said.

Chorus: As before.

There were no cops at ten o'clock as Shirley downed her eggs,
And none even at eleven: Shirley ate chicken legs;
She forget the cops at twelve o'clock, and she was saying her grace
When two gendarmes came screaming into daddy's place.

Chorus: As before.

The coppers in the driveway spoke in Neanderthal tones,
The fever to catch the Teddyboy coursed white-hot through their
  bones;
They muttered of burning his licence, their voices grew louder,
  and then . . .
Shirley and the Ted eloped, and were never seen again.

Chorus:

  Up to the car seat he vaulted. He jiggled the keys on the dash.
  Coughing, the engine turned over and Wham! he was off in
    a flash.

                                              Nigel Henery, 14

Epitaph

The marble gravestone told its own sad tale;
The lettering was clear and bright, as if
The mason's chisel had just cut
These terse and hollow euphemisms.
'Here lies . . .' I read; at once I turned my mind
To wonder why this life had ceased to be
A problem for the world it had just left . . .
. . . So recently.

There were the dates, and in between I saw
A dash, a shallow, narrow mark
Upon a white expanse, which said,
'He lived for nineteen years, and then
The world forgot him, all except
Those few who knew him, liked him,
And placed here the flowers which now
Are withering.'

He came into a world where he was told
A man must drink a lot, and smoke,
And call religion just a myth,
And treat the law as just a farce,
And drive as quickly as he can,
And preach a new morality he hopes will change
the world;
Or else
Be thought a little strange.

And so he did his very best to please
The world's demand for freedom and became
Its slave, and then its martyr when
He died within the twisted wreck
Of the machine they told him gave him thrills.

And now he asks that he may rest in peace,
In death which they all told him was the end;
So why the need?

D. Shannon

Sehnsucht

Are we wearing that look of fixed enjoyment
Usually kept for the cameraman's banalities?
Or could we be accused of looking sulky,
Or, worst of all, of looking older than we ought?
Perhaps we'd better plaster on the grease-paint,
And run about and break a window-pane.

We mustn't interfere with other people, we
Must leave the spineless and the sunken soul to rot,
Unfelt save for the smell of stagnant intellects.
And anyway, it takes all sorts to make a world,
And we're too young to understand such things.
Such interest in our fellows is unnatural.

Under the mockery of co-operation we
Subjugate originality to convention.
And yet beneath its suffocating blanket
We stir restlessly, seeking self-coherence.
Reflecting in our restlessness the chaos
Of the world for which we desperately prepare.

Hampered by hostility in our fellows
When we clutch at some unorthodox philosophy.
Accused of insincerity, of posing, and
Of intolerance, because we painfully
Strengthen our position, and refuse to change
Our views to suit some even greater bigot,
We grope our way.

Boy (1937)

Gift for a Child

I wish this child to have a gift—
Perhaps of love?

And if it is granted
Love may turn, its other side is hate
And hate brings men to war
And mothers mourn.

Perhaps for Art?
To paint a masterpiece in paint or words,
Inspire young fools to fight
And burn the dead within their doors!

Perhaps of intelligence?
This gift of life could lead a man to search
And find—a way of death
So vast, so terrible,
My earth may be destroyed!

Perhaps the skill to build?
But bombs and missiles with blasphemous names
Are built—
From building rockets to conquer space,
To building bombs to conquer man—
Even this gift may turn to sin!

Perhaps the gift to learn
To learn to live with other men
To learn to love the life we have
To learn kindness
And crush war and suffering with love—

So, love is the answer
The best gift
The gold of life.

                                      Robert Bramley, 15

Animals

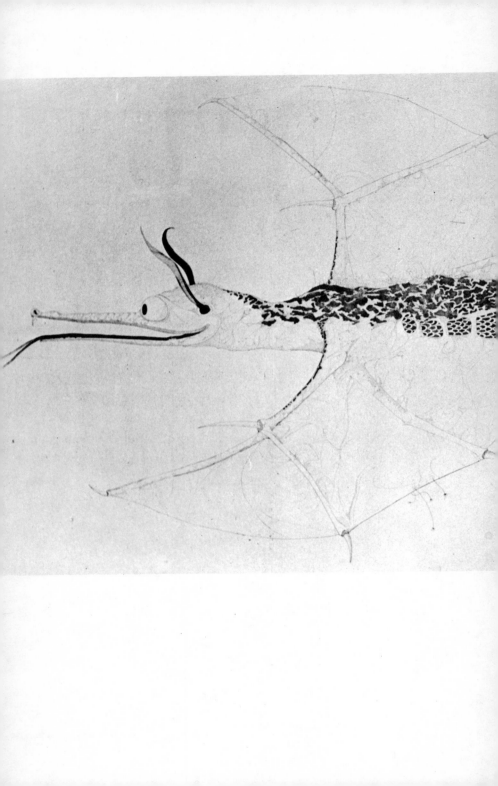

[47]

Dinosaurs

Some are big and tall
And some are small
Some are furry and some are curly
Some have trunks and some have none
Some are giants, some are midgets
Some are microbes, some eat leaves, some eat meat
Some lived in trees, and
Some on the ground
Some had long necks, some had small.

Some are still hiding in blocks of ice.

Andrew Cullup, 9

[48]

Water Wagtail

Water water wagtail
How many children have you?
Two asleep
Two with the sheep
Two to thresh the corn ears

Two asleep
Two with the sheep
Two to thresh the corn ears.

Olwen Clark, 6

[49]

My Newts

One night in thunder,
Two newts came to our back door to shelter
From the torrential rain and gusty wind;
I found them there when the rain had passed.

I caught them and kept them.
They are small and squirm when they are picked up.
Their stomachs and breasts are orange and black,
Pulsing with life.
They have four webbed feet and long shiny tails;
They are elegantly exact when they swim.

Out of the thunder night,
Came my black and orange dragons.

Clarissa Hinsley, 12

[50]

Snakes

Snakes—
As thick as drain pipes or as thin as shoe laces,
Wriggling, squirming,
Or coiled motionless ready to strike.

Snakes—
Slimy, slinking, slithering slowly,
Striking fear in everyone they meet
Striped ones, green ones,
Brown ones, orange ones, spotted blue and black.

Snakes—
I think snakes are prehistoric creatures
Left behind in a modern world,
Lying in wait for their time to come again.

John Manning, 11

[51]

Microscope

A microscope.
I looked through

A little Hydra,
  With a baby,
A bud on her side.
   She raised her tentacles
    And lowered them one side.
Beautiful thing.
   Over she goes . . .
A perfect handstand.
   And back the other side.
    Till she stands again.
Beautiful thing.
   How else could I see you
But through this marvel,
  Microscope?
A black tube,
  Some mirrors,
  Some lenses,
  A stand.
Uninteresting things,
Put together,
  Uninteresting things,
To make me see a
Beautiful thing:
  Hydra.

J. W. Chisholm, 12

[52]

Fieldmouse

Fieldmouse scampers,
Heart a-burning,
Machine rumbles,
Blades a-whirring,
Terror pushing,
Blindly faster
Thoughtless—heedless,
Stops—heart-a-busting

Machine rumbles,
Blades a-whirring
Bloody harvest.

Nigel Cullum, 15

[53]

The River Foss

There was silence all around me,
Except for the fall of the rain.
Suddenly she appeared, timidly,
As slim and elegant as a wraith,
Darting swiftly on her plashy way.

She was alone in the torrent,
Unaware of her impending fate.
Nearer, yet nearer, she ventured—
With one stroke she could have been mine.
Pity and her beauty made me
Linger a second too long: she was gone
With a flash, like a silver streak.
Only then I noticed the rain
That splashed and teemed; my clothes were
    drenched.
In widening circles the ripple spread
Where the stickleback had been.

A. Corfield, 14

[54]

Fishing

As I sit on the bank and the clouds move away
Releasing the power of the sun;
As the line tightens and my rod tip dips sharply
I lift the rod gently and strike, pulling back on the rod.

The brake on my reel slides off
And line shoots out quickly.
The fish twists and turns, dives and surfaces,
It gradually tires and I wind him in,
still wriggling, as I bring over the edge of the net,
Put my rod down and heave it onto the bank,
A full grown mirror carp.

Its brown body shines as the sun reflects on the slime
on the scales.
Its large brown body wriggles as I extract the hook
from its leathery mouth.
I put it on the damp, moist grass, wet with dew
And after wetting my hands, slip it back in the water.
It swims away with a flick of its tail,
To fight again another day.

J. F. S. White

[55]

Sonnet

O lovely O most charming pug
Thy graceful air and heavenly mug
The beauties of his mind do shine
And every bit is shaped so fine
Your very tail is most divine
Your teeth are whiter than the snow
Your a great buck and a beau
Your eyes are of so fine a shape
More like a christians than an ape
His cheeks is like the roses blume
Your hair is like the ravens plume
His noses cast is of the roman
He is a very pretty weomen
I could not get a rhyme for roman
And was obliged to call it weoman

Marjory Fleming (1803–1811)

Don't Go

I moaned and avoided taking you for your regular walks,
I hated to prepare that revolting meaty food.
I never found time to brush your black coat
But why, Queeny, did you run into the road?

I slammed the front door mumbling, 'Now where's
    that dog?'
There directly in front of me you lay.
Your eyes staring up to the cloudless sky.
Your jaws jarred open showing off yellow teeth.

Blood was pouring from the deep wounds.
Your once well-controlled ears flopped hopelessly into the
    shocking liquid,
Your nose, no more moist, but dry and hard.
I stepped forward shaking, my eyes filling with tears.

Then again I looked towards your body
You were twitching and whimpering, proving that you
    still had the tread of life.
A massive great lump appeared in my throat,
I started to cry.

I reached your body and crouched beside you,
Now, you were stiff, not uttering a sound.
I whispered, 'Queeny, don't go,'
Yet I recognised your death.

Patricia Buck, 15

The Eye of the Bird

The eye of the thrush
sees a worm,

and scaly legs
carry the speckled breast
to its quarry.

The eye of the swift
sees a fly,
and graceful wings
carry the forked tail
to a meal.

The eye of the owl
sees a mouse,
and silent wings
carry the large round eyes
to sustenance.

The eye of the robin
sees some bread,
and spindly legs
carry the scarlet breast
to a feast.

The eye of the blackbird
sees a crust,
and black wings,
carry the golden beak
to its object.

Timothy Travis, 13

[58]

Buzzard

King of the Moorland air,
Round and round he flies, mewing like a kitten:
Magnificent wings wide spread, tips like fingers.

Suddenly his rust-coloured body, caught by the wind,
Rises like a kite and over the field he glides,

Watching, watching, always watching,
Until a scuffle in the thick, wispery grass below
Catches his preying eye.

Wings back-swept and flashing in the sun,
As a feathered arrow he falls upon his prey.

He mews again, and his call is heard
By his mate gliding above their nest,
Hungry for the precious meat
To feed their squawking young.

                                        Tim Cawston

[59]

Chicken

I wandered from box to box,
Collecting the eggs from the hens.
Then I came to the one—
The one hen I always dreaded.
I looked at her as she turned her head and blinked.
So quiet, so calm.
Her red-brown feathers like the sinking sun.
I slowly put forward my hand,
And then she lunged, pecked and retrieved
Her fierce, sharp beak from my hand.
It bled and hurt.
I stepped back and looked at her.
So quiet now, so calm.
She meekly turned her head and blinked.
I needed that egg. The one to make the dozen
That went to the market the very next day.
But how?—How was I to get that white shell,
That yoke like the midday sun?
It was *her* egg; not mine to take away.
Should I risk putting my hand forward?
No— I wasn't going to have a chicken peck at me.
Savage! I thought.

I banged on the box,
    And rocked it from side to side.
Banging, banging; rocking, rocking;
Clucking, clucking; screeching, screeching;
Off!
Off she came, and there was the egg,
Smashed, and a yellow mess.

Richard Green, 15

[60]

Battery Hens

Each little hen
Each little cage
Each and every egg that's laid,
Are put in categories.

That's the life of the hen
The Battery hen
The shining cages
Hygienically clean.

The cruel, hard, short life
The brilliant lights
The spotless floor
For civilised well-mannered hens.

Sally Grant, 13

[61]

Cats

They sit neatly in little individual huddles
On the tarry black flat floor
Like old men put out in chairs on doorsteps
To get the last soft rays of evening sun.
Aloof.

Neither admitting the presence of the other,
They swallow softly, in grave content,
The orange light gleaming on their whiskers.
Complacent.
Unfocused eyes fixed straight ahead. Baskers
Lapping up the soft red sun.

Diane Bellwood, 17

[62]

Revenge or Pleasure

That blasted cat! Feline creature of misdeed
Crawling through the grass.
Ears pricked, nose down, short, black legs
Carrying the body and the brain,
Nearer, nearer to the pond.

The fish in lowly innocence swam,
As the cat moved to them.
In blissful ignorance of time and place,
They swam around the pebbly pool.
Danger was miles away from them.

And the cat had reached the pool
and its black paw stood raised.
He picked a fish. The paw flashed down
Like a guillotine
And then the fish was dead.

The hate welled up inside me
As I reached for my gun
The third this week the cat has got, but it will get no
    more.
Butt crashed into my shoulder as I prepared to fire
He came into my sights and . . . BANG!

But then remorse took hold of me. The cat just lying
    there.
A tiny trickle running from the hole. Blood!

Then nausea just hit me and as I sat down
I asked myself the question
Are revenge and pleasure one?

P. Kitchen

[63]

A Night Encounter with an Egyptian God

I wonder who hit it? And why?

Proud, defiant, it walks in the *middle* of the path,
Along the neat cement-squares.

> I pause, looking at it.
> It stops.
> We look at each other.

Shining eyes of distrust.

> No emotion inside me, only kinship.

Tentatively, my hand stretches out:
The lithe body arches away.

> A light just down the road,
> A street-lamp where a poet once wrote.
And so a thin shadow with pointed ears,
A head turned away.

It mistrusts me and all the human race;
> I chuck to it, on my knees
> And feel the cold, hard stone through my jeans.

> And feel the empty darkness around me
> With the shadow before me;
> And it becomes part of my mind.

The untidy, star-strewn, ragged-cloud-filled sky is forgotten.
Houses become non-existent—there are no people.

Just a faint rumble—a car whir.
    I kneel and hold out my hand.
Hesitantly, the shadow grows in my vision.
A small, triangular head thrusts into my hand,
And I am conscious of silky fur on my palm;
A wet nose.
I move my other hand—
Swifter than night brings fear, in fear, it curves away.
Soothing noises issue from my throat.

I circle it,
And the light brushes its face.
At last I see the eyes:
Huge young ones—beautiful
Eyes in a pointed head.
A god among creatures—
Yet also a stray like me.

                                    Tony Ross, 16

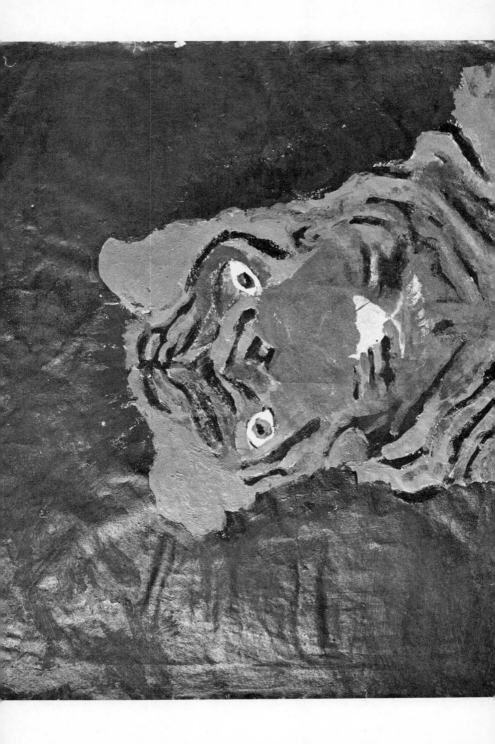

Elders

Sunday School Teacher

Mrs. Nunn
Please talk to me.
You always seem to pray
In Sunday school.
When I go to talk to you, you say time to pray
You give us our scriptures, when I go to say
What is the time
You say read the back of the scripture
Tig tig as you tap the side of a cup
Time to go home you
Say in a kind voice.
Now is my time to talk to you
God comes first she said.

Robin, 10

A Visit to the Staff Room

I knocked;
There was a pause;
Then, suddenly,
The door flew open.

'Please sir,
Have you seen my games sock?'
'There are some here.'
I stepped forward
Into the room.

Stop staring
At me,
Stop, stop,
I wished
To shout out.

Every eye,
Every chair
Was turned
In my direction.
But please
Just stop staring.

'Please sir,'
Addressing no one
In particular,
'It is not here.'

I looked up
At the faces.
'Stupid child,'
Someone whispered.

'Well, there is
Nothing I can do;
So out you go.'
'Yes sir.
Thank you sir.'

Me, a stupid child.
It's not
My fault
That my games sock
Got lost, I thought,
closing the door.

Boy, 11

[66]

Schoolmaster

Time is drawing the essence of you,
My old master, magnifying the clear,
Not the best; the best contradicts,
Left unseen, perhaps suppressed.

Memories, in the clear, white writing,
Very clear and very white, defying
You not to comprehend; in the mind
Moving precisely over the blackboard.

The impatient turn of your toecaps
Shone to a white black, reflecting
The wise old boiler in the corner,
Wheezing hazy assent.

The razor creases of your trousers
Stiff and dignified. Plunged in a pocket, the hand,
Ready poised with a vital understanding
Revealed at the crucial moment.

Coldness not kindness lingers on;
Your pride in knowing better, ever
Defeating wrong. And the sharp chill
Of a clear thing, gone.

                                        Jeremy Harris, 15

[67]

The Vicar

The Vicar is coming just after tea,
But he is not coming just to see me,
I think he is coming to watch the T.V.,
For we like the Lone Ranger and so does he.

                                        Carole Gardner, 10

[68]

The White Stick

Red bricks, grey slate, cream road.
My eyes ached,
Same old walls, same old houses,

Old churches, old shops, old railings,
Everything was old,
No grass or trees.
I was sick, for want of the country;
I looked around me.
My eyes were drawn
To a solitary figure, walking slowly.
I saw in the figure's hand a white stick.
Blindness.
I imagined the eternal blackness.
What had he done
To earn this mockery of man?
The figure turned into another street,
Tapping, feeling for the next shape,
Dependent on the white stick.
I wanted to help him.
What use was I? Just to show him the next corner.

Boy, 15

[69]

A Tramp

He had no were to go for every town, village and citys
    they would not let him stay.
For he had frightened the children.
It was his face that frightened them.
And his old coat with lots of patches.
He puts out his thin hand and asks people for food.
But they just run away because they are frightened.
So he had no were to go.

Girl, 10

[70]

The Historian

He is forever driving in reverse.
He backs his way along the narrow road
That drifts into a lane, without a map.

The wider motorways he leaves ahead.
And he can live a million lives at once.
It is his hand that signs away his life,
For he is both the baron and the serf.
So he can build an apple round a pip.
While we appreciate the growing flower,
He is more interested in the seed.
But driving in reverse is more secure,
For every sapling must have been a seed,
But every sapling will not be a tree.
Whichever way you go there is no map—
But what he searches for he knows exists.
The motorway may never be complete.

Michael Thompson, 15

[71]

Weddingdress

The dripdry weddingdress
And the amputated clock
In the cupboard, in the room,
Rustle, drip, tick, tock;
Mutter together in silence
Born from the world they mock.

The dripdry weddingdress
And the amputated clock
Quietly conspire to arrange
Future human livestock.

Stephen Baker, 18

[72]

Odd Man Out

He never fitted in well,
He never realised
The way that he dressed
Was not to their delight.

73

His clothes were hand-tailored
His hair short back and sides
His shirt was always clean
He even wore a tie.

He never fitted in well,
He never realised
The way that he thought
Was not to their delight.

His mind was his own,
He was honest and true,
It did not worry him to say,
What he thought of you.

He never fitted in well
He never realised.
The way that he worked
Was not to their delight.

With promotion in his path,
Promotion in his stride,
He worked hard all day,
From dawn until night.

He never fitted in well
He never realised
The way that he spoke,
Was not to their delight.

He never said slang phrases,
He never cursed or swore,
The perfect way he spoke
Made them hate him more.

He never fitted in well,
He never realised
The way that he lived
Was not to their delight.

A flat in St. John's Wood,
A big four-poster bed,
The way that he breathed,
Made them wish him dead.

E. Davies, 14

John: Menthol-Fresh

Lives in a house with a bigger garden
than his mother's—
gone up in the world.
Went down in Mr. Barrett's estimation
when he bought a red
Cyril Lord.

Settled down with the carpet though—
wouldn't be perturbed. Built himself a fire-escape
(first in the street)
and married a nice girl
whom his father liked.

Works in a bank,
but at weekends drives
to a pub two miles away
in a Ford Anglia
(local pub isn't quite him)
and knows the crowd,
who know him as Jack,
which makes him feel
a real bloke,
because he's John really.
Hates Jones because the Mail does.

Knows that Asians should
be barred
because his M.P. says so,
And his M.P.
of course
voices John's feelings.

Knows he'll die in thirty-five years' time,
knows his son will join
The air-force, fight a war,
become a bank-clerk

And die in sixty years' time.

                              Charles Hurt

[74]

Epitaph to a Failure

As a child he wandered and wondered,
As a boy he knew suffering and sorrow
And as he lived he learnt,
But learnt too late,
And his problems grew great,
Greater than he.

His ghost returned, by the will of a God,
To a timeless pinnacle where he was allowed thought
And where he sought long for a formula for life
And found none, for there was none to find.

Yet some who have seen say, 'Surely,
Surely that is not the ghost of a boy of yesterday,
Surely that is the spirit of a man of tomorrow.'

D. Mahadevan

[75]

Loneliness

The old man sat, tired, weary
The holes in his shoes were bigger now.
Another day watching, waiting, hoping
For youth, perhaps, or love.

The boy approached him, 'Hello Mister!'
The old man didn't move.
'You're dirty, old man, why are you dirty?'
The tramp looked down at his tattered clothes.

The boy looked into the deep eyes,
The street was reflected, the shops, the pub,
There were no people, the shops were shut,
And the wind blew away the litter.

The boy looked again,
It was dark, quiet, there were no lights,
The boy shivered and ran
Back into the busy highway.

Brian Gowland, 15

[76]

Old Lady

Looking into a neat drawer one day
She saw a scrap of old pottery,
When looking for something else;
The clay destroyed the tidiness.

Her nobbled old hands shook
And bent around her find.
She took it to her chair,
Her sitting chair, and sat.

She remembered.

The blowing of trees like
The murmurings of women over garden fences
Trembling together, swaying a nod of the head.
And standing on a heath threaded hill,
She had felt the days heat heave
And disappear, sinking into black ground.
The grass had been so clean from the valley.
Up there high above the city
The mud sucked at her foot's sole.

She remembered though;

The stone didn't fit into her files
Of old scenes in tinted photographs.
Her lips aren't as red as that now,
But her blouse remains sharp and white,
And her shoes are always clean.

Michael Hornsby, 18

Old Age and Youth

Yesterday I was young,
Today I thirst for youth.
Yesterday's future evolved
Into shadows of the past.
Years ago I laughed with friends;
Now, I sit alone with experience,
Gnarled, knotted hands search
For the money, the key, the ticket;
The world moves too fast,
And I too slowly.

They moan, they refuse to accept,
They want to be young again.
I abolish them in my mind,
Yet, I would like to understand them.
They live in the past, reality shocks them.
They value too highly experience
Gained in a forgotten era.
They are helpless, they crave for rejuvenation.
They are alone and the world moves
Quickly, and I with it.

Sarah Burt, 14

Country

Poem

And I went to a stream
And a merry stream
because it talks to me in a sort of whirling sound
And I call it a little way and it answers me back
And the ripples and pebbles dance together and say
'I wish I was you'
And the old trees stand to the breeze
still by the side of the river.
There are prickles and spikes
and old flowers that have blossomed
and died for years and years,
and the pretty old hedge that was there for ever
And perhaps long ago it still
was a lovely stream in England
Perhaps long ago there were willows
flapping in the wind.

Nicola, 7

Woken from Strange Dreams

Woken from strange dreams of summer;
tennis whites, thrush on summer lawn, with cricket's itinerant
drone.
Woken to moonlight, softly permeating cloud like a grey mantle
on the bright darkness of night,
a night, as in Cornwall you find, after similar dreams,
light reflected from water, with dark patches of cloud,
building up for storm,
and the far off surf on the cold rocks of granite—
seaweed covered, wreck haunted.
But no sea rolls in the distance, only in the shell of the mind.

And the dream-night stirs with the cool fresh breezes of spring
in a late summer guise
and the dream returns . . .

and a lone gull cries, far out on the withdrawing sea,
and a sad curlew cries, out on the far reaches
And the night, of occasional owl and scampering hedgehog,
dies in the summer breeze
And the thrush on the lawn still sings in perpetual summer,
and the tennis ball echoes eternally against itinerant crickets
all in a dream, image-made, of many long scattered lost
    summers,
and only the trees and the mist in the bright moonless night
capture my dreaming.

Richard Burnell, 18

[80]

A Broken Dream

It was a wonderful dream, but now it has gone,
Shivered in fragments, just as a broken crystal.
These have been halcyon days—Remember the sun
That coloured the countryside with a delicate pastel,
Setting the hedges afire with celandine stars
Which kindled the hawthorn into a sheet of blossom.
Marjoram burnt there too, and drab dead-nettle;
Perfume floated from them and down the lane.
Remember the sea—Ah! How could I ever forget it?
I find no words to express its thousand moods.
The sea on a stormy day—grim, black and furious;
Frowning with dark storm-clouds and belching thunder.
But, oh, how beautiful! And yet in Summer
As mild and gentle and docile as a kitten,
Green, calm, and liquid beautiful Summer sea.

Boy, 1936

[81]

The Pebble

Not a smooth, cold, sleek grey,
Superior pebble,
Nor a hot, rich, golden,
Exotic pebble.

But a humble, lumpy, bumpy,
Rigid lined,
Curved, streaked, spotted, dotted,
Stone.

A homely, kindly, bumbly
Sort of a pebble,
Like an old, gnarled, oak tree
In a forest.
Or a comfortable, mellow, wall,
Carefully built,
Lovingly formed, by an old old
Craftsman.

Francis Le Fèvre, 12

[82]

Stones

Limestone, Mudstone,
Marble, Clay
Coal and Chalk
With fossil gay
Sandstone, Granite
Coal and Clay,
Got into a muddle
Yesterday.

Limestone, Mudstone,
Chalk and Coal,
Fossils with a picture
Of a fish's soul.
Stones are the same
At day and night,
The fossils got a picture
Of an ammonite.

Chalk with fossil,
Sandstone gay,
Granite Coal and
Sandstone stary,

Rock with fossil,
Mudstone too
They like us
As we like them.

Rock with fossils,
Fossils with Rock,
Some are used for a
Great big knock,
Limestone, Mudstone,
Coal, Chalk too,
Some stones are Red
And some are Blue.

Simon Gibbons, 7

[83]

The Flint

Perhaps the gnarled and hairy paw of an early man
Held this flint as I hold it now,
Staring at the warm honey-coloured surface
Flecked with russety orange, crimson, black and cream.
Down in the flinty depths he may have looked
As I look now, through a glazed window at spots of
Misty white and orange.
He may have felt the rough surface, likening it to his own
    skin,
Gently stroking with a stubby fingertip
The smooth parts where he had chipped away the surface
To make some awkward tool.

Chloe Cheese

[84]

The wind wiseled passed the trees.
Pushing and puling the trees.
The water triying to rech it.

But still the trees remain.
The wind stops but still the trees remain.
Pepol diey but still the trees grow biger and biger.
Flower diey but still the trees remain.

Janice, 8

[85]

The Yew Tree

The yew-tree stands beneath the grey church wall;
Leaning tomb-stones its grim companions are;
Rooks round its gnarled trunk wheel and fall,
As the sounds of evening drift from afar.

Five hundred years has this grim old sentinel stood,
And in the days of long-bows and broadswords
Many an archer sought its wood.

Now, protected by its ancient right,
The yew-tree stands alone,
Black and bare, yet comforting in its might.

M. Clark, 12

[86]

Aspects of a Wood

How dark the wood, how strange the wood!
Shelter for the uncanny, shelter for the nocturnal
And the fatal owl, which warns of witchcraft
Performed in these dark and damp depths.

How pleasant the wood, how refreshing the wood!
The brown boughs and the golden leaves
Fluttering and dancing in the Autumn breeze,
Which lifts the crisp leaves into airborne flight.

G. Rawlins, 15

'The Evening . . .'

The evening is bright and the sky
is clear, but there is an atmosphere
of wickedness
in the lonely wood.
The trees take the shape of
human figures—
stretching their branches out,
trying to get hold of any lonely
human being
walking through the woods,
At that moment all eyes turn to a
girl who is walking through
the woods.
The trees circle round her.
They push her away as though
trying to tell her she shouldn't
impose on them.
She runs away but wherever she goes
she sees trees trying to catch her.
Suddenly
She trips and falls exhausted on
the floor.
She doesn't move—
and—
the trees are still.

P. Shirley, 13

[88]

Through Connaught

The massive slate-grey mountains frown
On bogs and neat mounds of turf
Piled high by black mirrors of water.
There is scrub and marshland,
Bordered by low grey walls

Stone on stone,
In parts worn and broken down by time or weather.
A lonely goat, tethered to a wooden stake, bleats mourn-
  fully,
And sheep, white dots, move slowly up the slopes
Past a tiny graveyard at the foot of a mountain,
Where only a few scattered headstones survive,
To mark where the bones of the long dead are laid.
The wind is whining and shrieking and screaming,
Like banshees at play, calling out.
The sky is dark and it rains, heavy droplets beating the
  earth.

Pauline Flannery, 15

[89]

Return to the Moors

The undulating quietness amazed me at first
And in bewilderment I searched for a hill
With an outline strong and comforting,
But there was nothing to take away the ache,
No towering height to awe into nothingness the void inside me.
My thoughts and hopes were centred on the scenes I loved
  and missed.
Where were the wild free moors, the gaunt bleakness
Of a beloved birthplace?
The air was soft, warm and peaceful,
Everything was green, fresh and clean,
The ideal setting for a happy, sheltered life;
But much as I enjoyed the soft breezes, they seemed strange
  and foreign,
For deep inside me were the winds of the moors,
Proud, untamed and relentless,
When I eventually returned from the fertile lowlands of
  the South,
I realised how much I had missed the moors, the wind, the hills.
Once again, I was able to climb almost to heaven
To lose my fears, doubts and suspicions
In the glorious freedom of the moorland world.

Girl, 14

Silence

Silence in London is generally a word that a teacher
uses to make a class quiet.
But in the country,
It is a word that explains the country.
The first thing you notice in the country,
Is the silence.
Happy singing of birds and creaking of branches,
Don't seem to be noticed.
All the noises of the country,
Seem to blend together like an orchestra,
Playing a woodland melody.
A funny echo fills the country.
There seems to be a breeze in my mouth.
My voice seems travelless.
My voice does not travel in the country,
for the trees grab it,
And make it a part of their symphony.
The trees rustle greedily when they clutch my voice,
Proud that my noise has become part of their song.
Sounds in London are jerky and bumpy,
My voice is full of stuffiness,
My voice travels far in London,
Not anybody bothers to take it,
My voice is too small to be important.

Trevor Dawson, 9

Midnight Swimmers

The cool sea air on the beach
The soft splashing of feet
Running nimbly nimbly down through the foam
Down, down to the cooling ocean
The midnight swimmers.

The small fire flashing, reflected
By the waves creeping up the beach
The beans spilling on the fire
Hissing like old steam trains
Shunting freight back and forth.

Raucous laughter of men and girls
Chasing up the beach
Falling to the sand by the fire
Slipping on bath robes
Drying their orange brown false tanned skin.

Eating sand beans
Talking, laughing, playing.

The beach is quiet now
Beneath the receding sea of high tide
The swimmers have gone back
To the nine to five jobs in Clarks assorted
    nuts and bolts factory
The last of the holiday makers
Next year fresh people will come
Eating picnics on the sand
But will I be here to watch
The midnight swimmers?

                                        Ian Turner

[92]

A Heated Moment

The weakly pushing wind has died away and left poised,
Shimmering on near horizons,
The image of a moment warmed to timelessness,
Containing frothing motion,

Smells of rising roads, absorbing heat with rough dull
    blackness,
Parted by the rhythmic thrum of wordless gossip,
Diffuse towards me, mingling amongst the sweetness,
Hinting at decay,
Of fresh-cut grass. Lying, drying,

A settled fly quivers motionless,
Silently springbound,
Siphoning the sweetness from an unheeding bottle-top,
Its silvery surface bent and dulled with fine dust.

A ripple begins at the far corner of the field,
And spreads like a golden blanket shaken by a soft invisible
    hand.
A watching village clock finds the time and chimes it;
The ripple has found me, hiding hopelessly from its chilling
    fingers.
Long yellow-edged shadows, thin and pointed dissolve into
    blunt grey veils.
I shiver, go inside, and shut the door.

                                        N. L. Rochford

[93]

The Ruined House

This house is the house of my childhood—
(I see it now, pressed into my mind so clear),
This was my life, my home, and me,
And now I come across this ruined house
That was me . . .
I can still see the country house,
That cobbled, winding lane
The village shop selling old-world food—
Nothing canned, all fresh from the greenhouse;
My old house was number 46 in the village.
Now with Council Planning, Land Development,
This great old house has its back broken,
Its very inner soul split open—
The rooms are exposed to the public gaze;
My home still stands,—in my mind,
Graceful, friendly,—
Now I live in a concrete block stories high;
I wonder if those all around me
Have memories of happy childhood
That lies lost for ever:

This block is number 46
In one of the many roads
In this modern town.

M. Ashford, 15

[94]

Remembering a Visit to Lanercost Priory

In the damp and windy land
Between two ridges,
The ruin stands.

All that is left of the church
Are the great sandy surfaces
Of walls,
The gaping black shapes
Which were windows;
Thick-slabbed, chilly tombs,
And a wind-broken silence.

The roof is a soft expanse
Of swooping storm clouds.
The floor,
A scythed lawn and a slippery path.

I remember four wet steps
Which rang in the empty dusk.
And on the stone coffins
In the echoing chapel,
There were no flowers.

Josephine Beck

[95]

Jaguar XJ6

Red shining car
In woodland glade,
How strange you seem!
An unnatural splash

Amid sombre hues,
Get back to your highway,
Your concrete panorama,
And leave nature to itself.

Richard Leggatt, 16

[96]

Riddle

I am man's old, old friend for ages,
And I am his ceaseless servant.
The carpenter, he shapes and trims me.
I am made in different substances.
Before he discovered me man had to drag his loads along.
I take my burden uncomplaining,
And I carry it smoothly, along flat ground and bumpy ground
  alike.
Man, in the future, may not have any use for me,
But he will remember me as an untiring companion.
My ways are uncovered, uncover my name.

Anton Roudette

Times and Seasons

[97]

The Mirror

The mirror saw her born,
It saw her grow up,
Saw her in her wedding dress.
It saw her grow old,
It saw her die in her bed.

Sean Laffan, 15

[98]

To Nettles

Nettles, of old I used to think
  No lot could be too hard for such,
Armed with your stings, and on the brink
  Of quarrel at the lightest touch,
And therefore, where I saw you grow,
I laid your fiercest chieftains low.

But now, when in the dark green shade
  Of woods I see you still and tall,
Or where some long dead man is laid
  By a neglected churchyard wall,
Whose grandchildren have never known
That he has lived, but I alone;

So many tales to me you tell
  Of knights and maids who here have met,
On days when this dead man was well,
  Your hasty temper I forget;
The rose herself must wear a thorn,
And not for nothing were you born.

Humphrey Devereux, 17 (1911)

The Skull

The chalky whiteness,
Crumbles after years
To earth and dust,
To make way for other creatures;
The swift that strikes the water,
The dragon-fly's bright blue wings,
The yellow bunting feeding her chicks.
They all prosper from this whiteness,
That now has turned to dust.

Boy, 14

[100]

Midnight in a Tube Station

Empty
Alone, I sit in a tube station.
A dog in an advertisement stares unnaturally at me.
I look the other way,
Nervously,
A paper bag rustles down the platform and into the tunnel
Noisily.
The dog stares at me
Blankly.
I turn to run but order myself not to, and sit down on a
    wooden seat.
The dog stares at me
Mockingly.
My train comes rattling into the station.
I board it—
Happily.

J. T. Anscombe, 13

And in the Night a Time for Dark

A space of time—a time to wait,
A time to pass the space of day,
And in the night a time for dark,
The reigning peace.

A space for peace—the cool beyond,
A peace of everlasting might,
And in the night a time for dark
The passive light.

A space of light—forgiving light,
A light that knows the upmost space,
And in the night a time for dark
And endless wisdom.

A space of wisdom—rising, rising
To a height that only the moon knows,
And in the night a time for dark,
A space to meditate.

Peter Davies

After Dark

It's bedtime,
Mother and father creak slowly up the stairs.
I get ready to go to bed.
The wind is howling.
The drunks pass by,
whispering and mumbling.

Milk bottles chime.

Dogs howl like death.

And now all the lights are out.
Only the street lamp shines
through the thin cotton curtains.
The house stands in darkness,
like a graveyard in the morning fog.
The windows crackle and the doors creak
as cruel winds quietly seek . . .
I switch off the lights, quietly as I can;
creaking, crackling and quaking, I nervously
climb the steep stairs,
afraid of disturbing my parents.
I jump into bed; springs clang and cackle
as I slide down the cool blankets.

Eric Kelsall, 15

[103]

Thoughts at Night

When one night, I looked at the stars
And saw their cold, unchanging faces,
I was lying in a field below the display
Gazing at the scattered salt of it all
And, wondering, alone, how it really began.
But my mind hardly worked with the startling idea
So I turned to my mate to speak of that day;
But I caught the light of his face upturned
And I held my tongue for I knew how he felt.

Bernard, 16

[104]

Evening

Pungent smell of the day's refuse, in dustbins.
Heavy air and heavier talk.
Stench of cold chips and vinegar,
Suspended in solid air.

Tea is over.
Children.
Ill fitting clothes and
Shuffling feet, kick a ball along the street.
Screams and lurid threats echo with laughter.

Long shadows cast by hideous, humdrum, hovels,
Fall blandly upon more such homes.
Row after row.
Blacker and blacker.
Noises compete with each other from house to house.
Television, clinking dishes and angry shouts,
Get to bed before I come and knock your
Flaming head off.

A baby whimpers,
Women in slippers and bedraggled hair,
Gossip incessantly.
Soon the night air pinches their fingers,
They recoil into the darkness behind closed doors.
Curtains are being drawn,
Only the lights remain alive in the night.
How much longer till dawn?

Christine Lodge

[105]

Night Tide

Shadows inch across the marsh,
Reeds rattle like dry bones,
Curlews cry,
Far away the owl does mope
And today must die;
But listen!
Ripples slap at restless boats,
The tide returns
And so does hope.

Jennifer Taylor, 15

Sunday

Dustbins surrounded by grime and soot,
  Dog cowering behind broken cardboard box
Which reeks with the smell of damp paper and must,
  Like the stench in the den of a fox.
Cats squalling in the cold of the night,
  Footsteps echoing down the black of the yawning alleyway,
Clouds obscuring the moon to dull the glistening frost,
No snow, no wind, no nothing, it's Sunday.

Christine Hemmings, 14

Friday night is my delight
And so is Saturday morning.
But Sunday night—it gives me a fright:
There's school on Monday morning.

January Morning

The crusted earth was topped with rime,
  While upright sprouts, rosetted green,
Intruded in the celery bed.
Among the crisp and brittle leaves
A tiny snowdrop hung its head,
  While from a hawthorn, spiked and bare,
Blackbird watched worm through beady eye;
  Rising from moss before wind, bitter and keen,
Are hyacinth leaves, spear-like and green.

Girl, 14

Lessons on Maths

(with apologies to Henry Reed and his 'Naming of Parts')

To-day, we have square roots and surds; yesterday
We had tangents and chords; and tomorrow morning we
Shall have angles, sine, cos and tan; but to-day
We have square roots and surds. Flowers
Sigh in the breeze and fill the air with sweet heady perfume
For they, they do not have square roots.

And this is the decimal point, the purpose of which
Is just vague and unknown, as you know. But we move it
Stupidly backwards and forwards. We call this mathematics.
And stupidly backwards and forwards
The drowsy-winged insects are flying in the meadows.
They call it lessons on maths.

They call it lessons on maths; it is perfectly easy
If you have sense and use your tables, for the roots,
And the sines, and tans of angles, and, of course, your brains,
Which in our case we have not got, and the laburnum trees
Lift their yellow lamps, and dance; and the black swifts dart
   rapidly downwards
For to-day we have lessons on maths.

                   Sonia Benson and Ella Whitfield (1955)

A New Start

On the first day of September,
Got up early in the morning,
Saw my uniform before me,
Saw my blazer neatly hanging,
From a hanger in the wardrobe,
Thought, 'At last the day is here now,
The day that seemed so long arriving'.

And I walked into the bathroom
Washed and hurried down to breakfast.
Breakfast over, time to dress now,
In my shirt and tie and tunic
Started getting very nervous,
As the clock ticked slowly onwards.
Started fumbling with my buttons,
Wished the clock would stop its ticking
For a second, for a minute.

One last glance into the mirror,
Fixing beret, fastening blazer.
Had to make a good impression,
At my first day in a new school.
Slung my satchel on my shoulder,
Said goodbye to Mum and Father.
Feeling rather strange and scared now.
In the cloakroom searched for faces,
Searched for faces of old school friends,
Found them in a group together,
Grouped together in the cloakroom.
Then I heard the school-bell ringing,
Joined the hoard of children walking
To the School Hall for the service.
Heard the Master start the service
Thought, 'At last the day has started'.

Hilary Steel, 11

[III]

Icy, Early Morning Frost . . .

Icy, early morning frost.
And crisp yellow leaves beneath my feet,
Green grass wet with frost and dew.
The mellow sun rising over the roofs of the trees.
The imprisoned fly in the silvery frost soaked web.
Cows peacefully chomping the green wet grass,
Occasionally casting an eye.
Mushrooms still in full view of the day.
The bleep of a car broke all this up.
And back to the hustle of life.

David Parker

Tenth Month

I wandered on the hills at dusk,
the far western sky bleeding over the gathering dark
in dying red, at the dying of day
and of year.
Wandered through the wraiths of sad shroud-mist
    winding
sorrowful through the old near-leafless trees,
gaunt and dark in their time of sleeping;
past timeless walls that once men built,
long ago when the sun shone warmly,
straggling lonely now, into a misty fading;
over the damp leaves, the depths of years
    beyond telling;
and across long grass, dew-wet in the early evening.
Somewhere a solitary sheep cried,
and the evening sang softly the song
of a distant stream.

    I felt the sorrow of a thousand autumns
    seeping in the mist over the ancient hills,
    and, mind cold-numb with body,
    feared, lonely, and left—
        —for I do not belong here, in the
            mourning of the land,
        and I must seek the lights of life, and
            forget that it is autumn.

The lights of life—cold concrete street-lamps
stand high, darkening the distant evening.
A motorbike belches fumes into the night
and fades red-lighted down the road.
Come, into the light, into the town,
and forget the saddening evening.
Come, to the traffic island,
the roundabout of life,
and look around you . . .
    A burst of beery laughter sounds
    from the open pub-doorway.

A crowd of youths and PVC girls
desperately age-seeking in the smoke-sodden
    night
wander aimlessly through the dingy street,
and yellow fog-strands twist about the
    shuttered houses.

The bitter East Wind whispers scraps of memory
in the gutter, where dead leaves rot,
and the world's filth gathers
in the time of dying.
And this, they say, is life
from birth to death
a lingering Autumn
The time of dying.
    So I must go again,
    flee from the bitterness of life
    to the quiet sorrow of the lonely hills
    where the ceaseless mind-rot of the unreal city
    is forgotten
    and the autumn mists drift endlessly
    into the silent Night.

                                        K. R. Moore, 16

[113]

A Walk on Christmas Morning

The slush of dirty feet.
A lonely seagull cries as it wheels,
Dark clouds linger overhead.

Here the party finished:
Empty glasses mourn on a coffee table
In the darkness of still-drawn curtains.
Spare rooms filled,
Five cars in drive;
Dining-room sleepers.
Here, a child awakes to find
That Santa Claus has been;

And there, a house left empty.
The partygoers are still asleep;
Drunken smiles adorn their faces.
Here, a wreath upon a door,
And there, a Christmas tree in window.
An early mother bastes the turkey.
In a lounge a family assembles
Exchanging presents, kisses and smiles.
In another, the deed being done,
Empty wrappings lie strewn around.

Small drops of rain ripple on the pond.
Even the dog senses the day.

Clive Wynn, 12

[114]

Winter Sun

The sun,
A watery disc in the pale, yellow sky,
Hung low over bare silent fields.
And the shadows of the tall grasses
Fell long across the still water of the river.

The trees on the bank were quiet,
And the leaves, in that waning, cheerless light,
Froze, and fell brittle and crinkling,
To be blown in chaff through the lifeless copse.

The raindrop ran along the bough,
And caused a momentary ripple,
Which sent a shiver to every corner of the pool,
As it entered noisily; then silence:
The twig dropped,
And the icicle distorted the horizon.

The sun,
Lower, fainter, in the dying evening light,
Cast fitful beams over the calm, deserted pool,
And the water mirrored the gathering clouds of night,
And the surface seized, and was a film of ice.

Gordon Picken

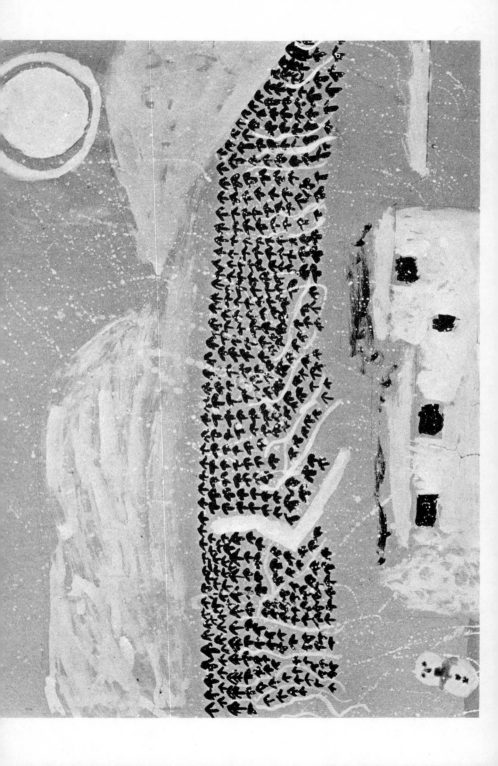

Snow Overnight

Slow, soft, and soundless the snowflakes sink down;
Now everything is snow like them; people stumble awkwardly
over slippery patches like flat-footed penguins.
Grass, paths, steps are smoothly sloping in soft curves and
spreading into one;
There are no longer stones, earth, plants, but only one
whiteness that hurts the eyes.
There is no sound: the world is like a clock that has stopped,
whose ticking is not noticed until it is not there.
Slow, soft, soundless,
And lonely.

The snow entangles trees, twists their knotty unevenness into
smoothness,
Merges them with all the other white,
Save where the great red winter sun
Tinges their topmost branches with warm pink.
The snow is everywhere, enveloping the trees with a white net,
And hanging the twigs of bushes with snow cobwebs.
A few people shovel snow or throw snowballs,
But they are like intruders in another world,
A world slow, soft, soundless,
And lonely.

S. R. Longwill, 15

Ie like the snow
falling
falling
down
falling on the tree
falling on the gras
falling on me

Vanessa Clarkson, 5

Contact

[117]

Bars

We climb on them
We play on them
We swing on them
We play round them
Bars are useful, Bars.

                                    Janet Stone, 7

[118]

Noise

I like noise:
    The huffing,
    The puffing,
    and buffing of a train.

    The teaming,
    and splashing,
    and streaming of the rain.

    The clashing,
    And bashing,
    And smashing of the plates.

    The making,
    The baking,
    And scoffing of the cakes.

[119]

Fishing

    You are sitting by the river,
Away from the hither and dither,
    You are fishing carefully and watching the float,
It strikes against the calm waters three times
    I STRIKE! blow, that one got away.

I watch it more carefully this time,
It goes right under.
   I STRIKE! blow, blow, blow, and blow again,
Back to the hither and dither.

Kevin Wood, 13

[120]

Library Checking

Sad,
To see the dust from a great book never opened,
To breathe in its unknowingness
With no desire to know.

Strange
To think that whoever wrote those thousand pages
Sat up all night by lamplight
At his passionate livelihood.

'No,
No one reads him now; he is out of fashion.
But once the printers printed him:
He was popular once,' they say.

Blue
Of the binding is faded into a musty grey,
And the gold-stamped arabesque letters,
Unreadable, are dumb.

Nothing
But the catalogue, in its neat impersonal order,
Remembers the obsolete volume
And passes on to the next.

Harriet Levine, 17

[121]

Journey Home

Collar up, head bowed low,
Groping forward for the dark, rectangular shadow
Through the mist of rain.

The shelter reached,
A solitary face waits with me, expressing bleak frigidity
Like the wind and rain.
The stone floor of the shelter is cold and glistening grey
As only stone can be.

Leaning against the damp back-boards
I look out through the mist to the desolate square,
Watching for the flicker of moving light.

Time passes, hopes dwindle.
As I settle down to wait
A dancing beam of light appears, then more lights behind it:
Closer and closer they come.
The ground rumbles as the great, luminous shadow heaves to,
but a few feet away.
And I feel the heat on my face
As I climb aboard and sink into the soft seat.

Feeling creeps back to my hands and feet,
And my ears pick up the sound of voices,
As I feel the hot air on my legs, and the purr of the fan.

I wipe the drops of water from the window,
And stare out into darkness.
The neon lights now flickering brightly,
Turning everything into a pool of light.
I can see the coloured lights on the window,
As I near my destination,
And prepare myself for the fresh ordeal.

The platform is cold, draughty,
But the warmth of the distant houses gives a kind of glow:
The bus stops, and with collar up I plod on.

I run, but the wind bites harder.
I walk, but the ordeal lasts longer.

I wait on the step, my toes numbed.
The door opens, in I walk
To a warmth that seems unreal!

Paul Ritson

The Highwayman

The train thundered over the bridge with iron roar
its lights flickered in the dark street below
and the white smoke slowly cleared.

Once again the rain filled the air
pouring, pelting into the swirling road
dashing white spray into the freezing wind
and torrenting into the gutter.

We rushed up the cascading steps;
the gale stung our cold, wet skins
and smarting faces; blinded us.

We waited under the drumming canopy
soaked and shivering;
the wind blew ripples on the glistening platform.
And a limp, wet newspaper
wrapped around my feet.

We no longer have to wait for trains;
we have a car.
But how I long to be on that platform
exposed to the rain and cold
when I'm slouched in the back of that stuffy hole
hot and sweating, head aching
feeling sick and empty.

Nigel Hall

[123]

Judo Contest

The novice grades had finished;
Now for the experts.
The tense, hot crowd around the mat
Hushed as the contestants appeared.

Strong, heavy men.
Black Belts.
Like jungle-cats they padded on to the soft mat.
The ceremonial bow. The starting position.
Like an explosion they started,
Concentration marking their features and feelings.
Their vice-like grips
Sliding along the damp, bare arm.
The agony of thinking many times faster than
    normal—new attacks
Different counters.
Their breath comes in short, sharp gasps
Like a vigorously-worked pump.
Their vision,
Distorted by the small streams of sweat that flowed
    down their bodies;
Their ankles,
Sore, stinging from the attempted ankle trips.
Quite suddenly a face lights up!
He can feel his opponent moving in
To throw.
A side-step.
A whip-like movement.
He's down—only his keen reflexes
Saved him from injury by breakfalling.
The bow of honour.
They quiver with relief and their release
From the nervous stress and strain.
Silently, exhaustedly,
They slip off the rough, damp mat,
To rest and recover.

J. Rathbone, 16

[124]

Train Journey

Against the jolting of the wheels
The morning papers shake
An eye, made bloodshot by the sun
Peers over Vietnam News

The Times then crumples; there behind
A common paperback
This idiot frontage should receive
Our scorn or censure; but
The choking dust and lazy heat
The stolid tramp of the train-beat
The peaceful country, green and neat
Just make me yawn and want to laugh
In pleasure.

William Parente

[125]

Street Accident

Round bell, angry horn spiralling the air,
Frightening cars and buses from its smoking path,
Blinking its one blue eye in anticipation,
A cross in blood on its cream antiseptic flank,
The ambulance comes whistling, to take away
The wreckage of man from the bundle of cast-off matter;
Metal and rubber can wait for another day.
People stand around to watch this awesome meeting,
People from nowhere, magnetised ever by
Misfortune; photographers flash in their cruel joy,
Policemen keep the crowd from going insane,
Dancing on the wreckage, glorying in their blessed
Ransom from death by others' sudden fall:
This time death has passed them closely by.
Safe for a few days now; it isn't likely
That fate will pitch on them as well, to add
To those marked down for a death this week on the road;
And as to those who have, it's just too bad.
For chance should now go chasing another fox,
And lightning won't strike again—yet—in this same place:
Or if it does, it will only be very bad luck,
And the rest will receive
Yet another reprieve.

R. H., 17

Thirty Coins

The dead have been carried down,
And on the wind-swept mountain-side
Peace reigns. But no quiet peace:
The wind howls as we walk up.
Thirty feet higher and lives would have been saved.
As we near the top we see burnt wreckage,
Remains of a giant white bird.
Thirty coins lie in the snow.
The ashes of their purse have gone,
Blown away.

If the bird could rise again,
Into the sky like a phoenix,
Thirty people would live on,
And thirty coins would be spent.

Richard Belding, 15

The Number Eight

The number eight
Rolled to a stop by the concrete shelter.
A negro embarked,
And people stared for a split second
Then returned to their talking,
But more quietly.
He sat beside a woman, who turned away
To stare with cold embarrassment through the window.
Suddenly a little boy turned in his seat,
And asked, 'Why are you black?'
''Cos I spend a lot of time in the sun,' replied the negro.
No-one laughed.
He smiled.
Then sat, ashamed.

Alan Rodgers, 17

Poem of Waiting

Clattering cups, blaring records,
Nervous minutes tick on by.
Heavy transport lumbering past
But no motorbike sound to grate on ears.
Robot fingers stub out cigarettes.
Coffee swirling in cracked cups
Loud male voices, jeering, laughing.
More pop records to jar the nerves
Turn the thing off, quickly, now
He won't come back
But what do you care?
And still no sound of motorbike,
Unaware of elbow jabs
She stumbles to the door,
The night and road for once is quiet,
Red cigarettes burn in the dark
As regular as neon signs
A noise—Thank God—he's here at last
The quavering beams prick the road
A grate of brakes and skidding gravel
Goggled eyes, his windswept hair
Kisses of relief, laughter, talk of motorbikes.
Protective arm around her shoulders
She sits quiet and tries not to think
Of the day when motorbikes will
Not be heard, or his face not to
Appear at the door, but the stricken faces of his friends.
Was it all worthwhile—the
Unsteady world of neon signs and motorbikes?

Barbara Lindley, 16

The Cocktail Party

I am getting old,
My limbs are stiff
And my feet are large and painful.
(I will have to buy new shoes.)

All I do is wander like a tame dog.
Saying, 'Good evening' to everyone who looks my way,
(I sometimes wonder who they are)
And, 'No thank you' to the waiter with the drink
As I cannot give him a tip.
Sometimes I see someone I know
And wonder how they got invited,
And what they will say to so-and-so
Because I am here.
Now and then I wish I was younger,
But I think of my 'dear' wife
And forget these thoughts.
It was my wife who brought me here,
'To keep up social relations,' she said,
But she really meant social gossip.
There's a man I know, sprawled over the bar,
Poor chap!
Ah, well! . . . Here comes my wife.
Do not say she is going home.
She is.
Got to get her beauty sleep.
(She will be up all night phoning her 'grape-vine'.)
Here comes the host to say goodnight.
(I do not know who it is, but it does not matter.)
Soon I will be able to take off my collar,
Start the old engine up.
And these wretched shoes.

Jennifer Rowe

[130]

Ghosts

The dark sky,
The full moon,
A short cut through the graveyard,
A low cloud comes rolling in,
It shrinks into a ball,
Then parts extended
To look like a man.

They turned and ran,
Eyes in bushes,
Eyes on nowhere,
Smoke, devils' smoke,
Dead men rise,
The sign of death.
Then, a flash in the sky,
Rain, they don't like rain,
They disappear,
And you are safe,
For now.

Boy, 13

[131]

Nobody Comes

A hand on the door, again
The sharp rattle of the lock,
Or is it the wind, unwittingly
Striking the boards? The clock
Squatting unnoticed on its perch
Wakes and strikes, the door replies.
Tensed by these nightly sounds, my ears search
The rumoured dark: nothing certain
But a hint of footsteps on leaves,
Approaching or passing by? The curtain
Trembles, and if there was a candle
It would mark the hostile air;
The noises stop, and Nobody is there.

And in dreams follows at a distance
Always slightly out of sight;
In loud forests hidden by trees
When storms wreck the foaming night,
On the road, behind a curve.
Then the reins of panic tighten
And driven to run I swerve
Down a strange path to a safe
House, knowing its door will not open
In time, and when I turn to face

The breath on my neck, I know,
Thereby completing the nightmare
That Nobody will be there.

And now a scratch at the window,
A hand drawn across the cool glass
Tries to break in. Slowly I move
To pull back the curtains, pass
The crowing clock with its wise
Informed laughter, and tear them wide;
I drag the darkness with my eyes
Knowing that Nobody stalks the night,
Only the unconcerned trees stir
In the room's hard split light.
Then nearer something forms,
Quiet hunter faces hunted with despair:
My cold reflection fixes in the air.

Richard Tibbitts, 18

War

The Coming of the Norsemen

The war horns brayed,
Brayed like the sound of the
Breakers crashing upon the cold
North-beach
Brayed their message to all
Who would hear,
To all the world.
And the Norsemen answered,
Answered all who would
Question their power,
Their berserk madness.
They crossed the wild foam-flecked enraged sea.
The dragon prows ploughed
Through the grey-green sea.
A hundred prows, a hundred times three.
Seeming in number to rival the stars
In the sky.
So they journeyed along the gulls way
Until they saw the smooth untroubled
Waters of the Humber.
With a roar of triumph
Unmolested by the cowering guiltless
Men of the fields.
No man stood before them,
No man had the courage to resist.
Blackened charred ruins of what
Had once been villages
Lay in their wake.

Michael Robinson

Dublin 1916–1967

The traffic ground across the Liffey into O'Connell Street.
I stood and watched, detached, the thronging crowds,
The bright shop-windows and the screaming neon signs.

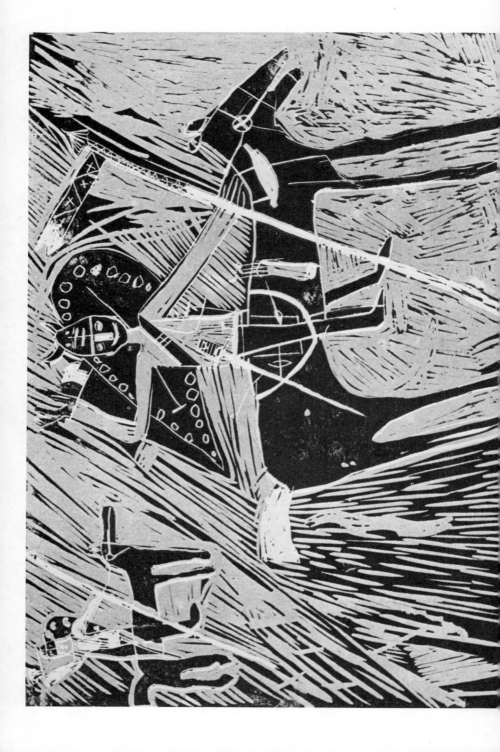

Here in Corcaigh Street, late Coronation Road,
The British regulars raised barricades
Of broken furniture and firewood.
And there, behind the churchyard wall, the rebels crouched
Desperate, outnumbered, mechanically firing
And loading and dying, as squadrons of horsemen
Thundered forward in the final assault.
There by the bridge on College Wharf a battery of field-guns
Sent shell after shell into the General Post Office
Until inside, charred timbers, scattered corpses
Were all that remained. But the flag still flew.
I fingered the marks of the bullets in the heavy pillars,
Lumbering skywards in stilted Victorian Classicism,
And I watched the people, happy and empty-headed,
And I thought I understood.

Hugh Clifton

[134]

The Unknown Warrior

Clear against the evening sky, the glorious
Hero there, sits fearing every sound.
He feels no joy of patriotic calling—
Dulce lies, he knows not where. Decorum
Never enters. All he cares is Mori!
Not for any country. Does he know it?
Can he tell it? Millions homage by his
Grave will pay. A crash, a roar, a shriek, and
Funky Private Bridle was the warrior.

M. Z. B, 14.5 (1936)

[135]

Epitaph on a Churchyard

Blackened trees, leafless bushes,
Leaning stones and careless thrushes
That sing above a windswept path
Where leaves rustle in the aftermath
Of the sleeping twilight days before
A sleep-walking nation went to war.

Perhaps the church had a grey slate roof, watched over
By rich green conifers which shadowed the worn-down step
At the door. Maybe the bark of the trees was red
On one side, greened on the other. Probably the
Choirboys whose voices were breaking did not realise
That they would be parting quite soon for trench, ship, sky—
Where there are medals for those who do not die.

I cannot tell.

And then I suppose that everyone's shirt was white,
That the swinging gate that must have been there was white,
And that the cricketing vicar's practised hand was white
When I was carried in there to be christened—in white.

But I know
A bomb fell.

Beneath a globe of turquoise sky,
Barred with long frowning purple clouds, I
See only the wind in the green sea
Of nettles, whistling over the rubble and the
Burnt rafters. One relichened wall
Stands, only unnoticed, to fall.

Boy, 15

[136]

Where was God?

And where was God
When war broke out?
Where was he, not to hear them shout?
Where was God when aloud they cried?
Where was God when they died?
Where was God when blood was spilt?
Was he asleep
Or was he aware
Or was he fighting the devil?

D. Williamson

[137]

Hiroshima

Noon, and hazy heat;
A single silver sliver and a dull drone;
The gloved finger poised, pressed:
A second's silence, and
Oblivion.

Boy, 15

[138]

Hiroshima

We helped
in a way.
New buildings, a new town.
New people . . .
We helped in a way.

Hiroshima, a new place.
The old remember,
they're here and gone.
We bombed the people, alone.
No soldier died in
Hiroshima.

Alan Bray, 13

[139]

A Child Killed in War

I was one who became Nothing
In the sharp, bright Sun,
Where the heat-haze confusion
Blurred,
And only the burning remained.

C. E. H. Farrands, 17

Refugees

Dragging feet, slurring along an unknown road,
Dull eyes deadened by life-long fear,
Blank faces, suspiciously regarding authority,
For authority killed their loved ones;
Drove them from their homes to wander in a foreign land,
To shelter in cardboard shacks provided by some friendly
    organisation.

Trudging desolately away,
Leaving all they know,
Clutching their few possessions
Pathetically bundled together.
Children squalling, frightened.
Families fleeing, with their lives
Held in the hands of warriors.
Here are the sufferers from the senseless wars,
The remainders of war's destruction, the ones who are
    perpetual reminders
Of all that man creates in order to destroy.
The hopeless ones—the refugees.

Girl, 13

Cyprus

Two hearts bitter as the lemons on the hills,
Two souls troubled as the waves around the isle,
Two dead men peaceful as the doves among the myrtles.

Friendship broken like the panes of glass,
Love lost like youth's joys in the past,
Tempers sharp-pointed like the isle.

Guns smoking as the chimneys of the cottage,
Blood flowing like wine drunk in calmer years,
Ruins of war and not of gentle age.

John James, 15

Vietnam

Guns, shouts, noise,
The Americans in their smart uniforms,
Hustle the thin, limp, ragged peasants into the shelter
of the trees.
A child screams,
No-one seems to notice, they are all fleeing in
fear, of death.

At Saigon,
The American hospital is full of maimed men,
women and children.
Children and babies who know nothing of Communism,
die of hunger,
And the merciful death of a bullet.

The Vietcong are savage,
But so too are the Americans with their machine
guns, bullets and tanks.

*why are the
A. savage*

Spare a thought for the orphaned child,
Left alone and being torn in two,
By Russia, China, me and you.

J. Sparks, 15

Originality

Even if I strive to think
Think of something original
I couldn't say it anyway
That hasn't been said before,
By you or any other
I couldn't tell of all the hate
Nor all the terror of the innocent victims of war
Nor of the size and shapes of things
That stand between man and man.

Nothing can be original
Not even death
The world's come to an end
We know what's coming next
And it won't be original death
Even death by the atom bomb
Was thought of fifty years ago.

R. Bonfiglioli

[144]

I, the Jew

I am he,
He that lives, he that suffered.
He that suffers.

I am of Man,
But Man, since my birth has harmed me.

I came of age,
And was exiled from my home.
I spread over the world,
And the world repelled me,
Repels me.

. . . .

In Spain, some centuries I lived in peace
Then the Inquisition.
'Live—Christian. Die—Jew' they said.
And I made a good fire, for a good cause.
'Love your neighbour' they used to say.

France and England housed me
For heavy rent.
And brave Richard the Lion Heart
Before going on his noble pilgrimage, said
'Love your neighbour my good citizens,
And kill the Jew'.

So my blood poured
While Richard the Lion Heart
Fought for my land.

And then Germany, Poland and Russia
To the Ghetto.
—Four dark walls and as many dark streets.
I wore the yellow star
And lent money.
I was spat upon and kicked into the gutter,
'For eating the fat of our land',
They said when I was rich. And
'For not paying the Jew Tax'
They said when I was poor. And always
'For being a Jew'.
How they loved their neighbours!

Passover, my festival of freedom
I spent hiding from the mobs,
Who cried, 'The Jew uses our blood for his wine
He kills our children'.
And my blood poured
For my neighbours who loved me.

And one day a mob entered the gates,
The gates in the walls in the Ghetto.
And they plundered, and robbed, and raped and killed
And more mobs came,
Until the streets of my Ghetto
Stank with my blood.
But it gave my neighbours pleasure,
My neighbours who loved me.

Then came a new idea from Germany,
'Keep Germany clean, and kill the Jew'.
And they starved me
And they burned me
And they gassed me
And they made hygienic soap from my guts
And explosives from my body.
But Germany was disinfected, of me.

. . . .

Germany is crushed—and I crawl on.
Behind me a dark, dirty past.
As they polish their weapons against me.
And I crawl on,
And I suffer
And I live.

                              Michael Lowry, 16

Love

[145]

The Departure

Goodbye, he called
Goodbye, I said
The puffs of smoke came out of the engine's funnel
And it slowly pulled out of the station,
I suddenly hated that big iron monster
For taking my friend away,
I felt that I could pull it apart
With my bare hands.

He called again
But as I called back
The sound of the engine drowned
My words.

Peter Fourniss, 13

[146]

Oh Isa why do not you write
I'm out of mind when out of sight
I am afraid your dead and gone
And thus I do begin my moan
O miserable unhappy child
To lose a mistress meek and mild
With all the graces which adorn
I wish that I was never born
I cannot bear the thought and Oh
Indeed I wish it was not so
Thine eyes with luster will not show
And in the grave where it is drere
Thou shalt be laid a lady fair
It fills my heart with great despair
Indeed I now must say adieu
Both to Isabel and you

Marjory Fleming (1803–1811)

Youth

We stand together
Hand in hand,
He so earnest, so concerned
In my tears.
Why do I cry?
What questions he asks!
Why do I cry?
How can I tell?

I could have laughed,
I could have stood
and screamed
at the dull drips of rain,
his fond stupidity,
His wiry hair,
his youth.
But no,
I stand and cry.

Caroline Dalton

The Lost Love

I knew a boy, he was so gentle,
he loved a girl who loved him not.
She looked gentle, but she was not,
I loved him, but he loved me not.
He was so gentle.

All he loved was his dog,
and the girl in his class.
We have fun,
but I do not know if he likes me.
He was so gentle.

I loved him, how much I cannot tell him;
he would say you do not.love me,
and laugh.
He was so gentle.

Sandra McGhee, 14

[149]

To Her

I love to feel you close to me.
Warm,
Receptive,
Not just as a thing,
A pleasure machine,
But as another person
Feeling,
Breathing,
Thinking independently.
You suffer,
The same stresses as I
But I forget.
And treat you as a thing
And spoil it all.

P. K. Gilroy, 13

[150]

One Afternoon

It was a most beautiful
afternoon.
The rich smell of the long green grass
was overpowering.
And we lay in the long green
grass,
And felt the soft caress of the blades.

It was so quiet
we could almost hear the billowing of the
clouds,
as we lay in the long green grass—
hand in hand.
Then we kissed
quickly.
And for a moment we were able to leave
this world of hate and
sorrow.
Then we kissed again
and this time you kissed hard and greedily
in the beauty and
quiet
of the afternoon and the long green grass.
And a feeling of nausea
came over me—
because you had spoilt it all by being
greedy.

Boy, 16

[151]

For Ever

Rain falls heavily on the roof
And the wheels hiss on the road.
Lights rush by
Scattered by little running droplets
Into a million stars
Against the black night sky.
Town and countryside become blurred
As mist on the windows
Gradually turns the coach
Into a cocoon
Dimly illuminated.

The sound of voices
And the noise of the engine
Are distant.

Here, the background music
Is the song of the road and the rain
And the lighting
Is one little bulb
Glowing feebly above the back seat.
And you and I are the main characters.

We seem alone in our cocoon
Your head on my shoulder
My arm round your waist
Warm hands intertwined.
Your dark hair is my horizon
Silky soft against my cheek
Hiding your pretty face
Like a black veil.
When you speak
Your voice is soft and slow
To match your movement.

The bus journeys on through the night
Fighting the pounding rain.
For ever.

Richard Clay, 17

[152]

Message to a Runaway

Are you happy now
The one big question is answered,
The decision is made,
And the journey undertaken?

Always look forward;
Never regret your decision,
For regrets are nothing,
But you always have the future.

Echoes of weeping
Disturb the shadows of loneliness,
Whispering sorrow
Through the empty streets.

Be happy in the thought
That I understand your action.
Only duty held me,
And holds me from following.

This is my gift—
A message which will never reach you.
I sing to the air,
Which comforting, cannot hear me.

Angela Bowles, 17

[153]

Poem

Winter time's not bad,
But it's cold if you're alone.
It wouldn't do to break
With her just then.
To leave her in the Spring
Is sacrilegious;
Time never was, but Spring
Is the time for those like us
Summer days have a lazy convenience
That would be wasted separately;
And anyway, it's far too hot
To argue with her heatedly.
That leaves Autumn, with Autumn leaves
To go tumbling in together,
And, sharing bite for bite,
The fruit tastes sweeter.
I couldn't part with her then, either;
So it seems I'll never leave her.

Richard Boulton

[154]

How Long

How long is it now,—a year or more?
No matter. Time's not important
And neither are you, surprisingly.

Although you haunt me,
You're undesired and irretrievable.
A bright, green leaf blown far away,
Turns brown and slowly dies.

What is important
Is the height of love I reached for you.
Even its memory's stronger
Than any love I have known since.
I wonder if you left me incapable of love?
Did the shock of your desertion
Turn my eager heart to ice?

If so, then it must melt,
With warmth from outside and within.
How long will it take,—a year or more?
No matter. Time's not important . . .

Kathleen Woosey, 18

[155]

There was a Time

There was a time when,
If I but chose to touch your cheek,
    You would kiss me.
A time when the sea was blue,
    birds sang, bells rang, blue-bells grew.
You loved me then, and I loved you.

But waking
We found the Golden Days had gone.
Winter had come, and no sun shone.

Our love warped with the weather.
In winter it was thrown away—
An old record: it would not play.

Thus, we were bound to part,
  as part we did.
We played the game of hide and seek
  and hid.

Sally Rosser

[156]

To L

O you my other self my other I,
The only other one with whom I share
Trivial things: how different can you be!

You who alone can understand my cry,
Who, alone, can sense my every care:
Yet can I never grasp you but you flee.

I do not understand your frightened lie;
The quicksand of your soul which, like a hare,
Dodges and feints, yet always scorns my plea.

So must I still not reach you, still not tie
My common bond to yours; can we not pair?
Laws stand between us, like a gaunt decree:
Your house of grim brick, mine of tarnished gold;
And yet our paths join—at infinity.

J. K. Kolaczek, 17

[157]

Sunday Morning

Lying in pools of pale winter sunlight
and sinking in seas of warm white sheets,
I watch the hills of his body rise and fall
as he blows his clouds of cigarette smoke up,
a soft grey mist in the goldlight.

Listening to the piano concerto rippling
clear and tinklinglass notes,
spilling into the sunlit room and softly dying
so, I watch him smile back to sleep.

Lucy Annan

[158]

Feelings

I listen to him intently,
He's asking me to do it,
But I can't.
It's easy for him, so easy,
But I have to bear the pain
The aching, the thumping in my womb.
Just so he can have a bit of fun.
And yet I want to, because I love him,
But does he love me? does he want me?
What will he do after?

I tell him no and he presses against me,
Begging me to
But I can't, I couldn't stand the heartache,
If he left me.
He's angry, I plead with him, he's cold.
He walks away and leaves me sitting,
And yet I'm comforted because I know I've done right
He didn't love me.

Daryl Ball, 16

[159]

How, at the age of twenty-five, I shall find true happiness

Somewhere,
lives the pretty girl
I shall marry.

Somewhere,
stands the church
where we will be photographed
with all our relatives
and great Aunt Ada.

Somewhere,
is the bank
which will give me my mortgage.

Somewhere,
is the coastal town,
where we will go for our Sunday drives
in the middle of winter.

Somewhere,
when this happens,
I shall take out my brain,
solemnly bury it,
and read a funeral service over it,
for I will no longer need it.

Paul Sutton, 16

Coming to Terms

Juggled and Muddled

I've got a skipping rope that's
Juggled and muddled and twerled
around. I've got a puppy I juggle
and muddle his tail, he bites
and growls, I love juggleing and
muddleing and twerling
everything. I twerl the tape
measure and daddy gets cross.
and daddy sends me up to bed.
I juggle and muddle my bedroom up
until it's a mess,
I juggle and muddle my dolls cloths
up I love it.

Barbara, 9

The Balloon

Bright leaves, Nature's pride and joy
Slender innocence,
  Hanging like rain on the bough.
Then, like a burst pipe expanding, lung-like
  Aerobatic displays, bounding on air,
Hovering feats of twisting.
  Then a child's heart is broken,
Nothing can replace it.

Boy, 11

[162]

The Wide, Wide World

The world is wide
Theres no place to hide
There is no way out
I look round and about
I go to school everyday
And learn my sums the proper way.
Then when I go out to play
I try to get out another way
But now I know theres no way out
All though I still look round and about.

Louise Hillyer, 8

[163]

Temper

Temper is a red hot hate which glows inside you
It takes over all love and boils it
And flows through your body like bolting lightning
It sticks in you like knives of thunder
And feels as if you want to destroy
And to make a revenge which you cannot make
To fight when you cannot fight
And to rise against your enemies
But this is the abominable that is not visible to us
But all we can see is a stubborn way of revenge
This leads us astray to wander forever.

Clyde Clarkson, 11

[164]

Anger

I strike very quickly, suddenly coming,
But spread through a body slowly.
I warm, simmer, rise and boil.

Up into cheeks I creep,
Veins bulge, pulses quicken.
From mouths come insults—
Better unheard.

I bring about blows.
Curses and cutting remarks,
Grimly set jaws,
Attacks and lunges,
Stamping of feet
Pulling of hair.
There are ugly displays—
Better unseen.

But when battles are fought,
Blows are forgotten
Hands are shaken
And prides once wounded, healed.
I simmer down—just warm;
Then cold, I disappear—
Better unknown.

                                        Michael Price, 14

[165]

Oh Isa pain did visit me,
I was at the last extremity;
How often did I think of you,
I wish your graceful form to view,
To clasp you in my week embrace,
Indeed I thought I'd run my race:
Good care, I'm sure, was of me taken
But still indeed I was much shaken,
At last I daily strength did gain,
And oh! at last away went pain;
At length the doctor thought I might
Stay in the parlor all the night;
I now continue so to do,
Farewell to Nancy and to you.

                                    Marjory Fleming (1803–1811)

[166]

'I like you—do you like me?'

I wish to say I like you,
But I know not how to say
Or express myself openly,
There isn't any way.
Am I shy or confident
And am I nice and gay?
Though maybe I am ugly
And will presently decay.
I admire you personally
But what of me and why?
Tell me what you think of me
In your expressive way.
Do you really like me?
If you do then say!
Though perhaps you don't prefer me
And will push me on my way.

Simon Griffiths, 13

[167]

Me

What am I?
  A boy.

Why am I?
I can never arrive
At a satisfactory
  Answer
As to why
  I am.
But there must be a reason,
For without a reason,
What is the point of
  Me

Being around to eat
    Good food
And using up
Useful space.

So,
Why
Am I?

[168]

Child or Adult?

Am I a child or an adult?
No! Not a child now—my dolls are gone;
My dream world has rippled away.
I am tall, I understand adult talk,
But does that mean that I am an adult?

Am I an adult or a child?
No! Not an adult—I couldn't look after myself;
The understanding is just not there.
I pay a half fare on a bus to school,
But does that mean that I am a child?

Am I a child or an adult?
No! Not a child now—it's not a teddy I love;
His cherished position is taken.
Just because my toys have lost their value,
Does that mean that I am an adult?

Am I an adult or a child?
No! Not an adult—I do not see
The reasons for adult disputes;
I am safe in non-understanding,
But does that mean that I am a child?

Well, am I a child or an adult?
No! Not one or the other now;
One pace in front of childhood,
And one behind an adult.
Soon I shall stride into a new world,
The world of adult life.

Margaret Lawrence

[169]

Growing up

No longer
The welling up of condensed sorrow,
The trickle of warm, saline beads
Mounting . . .
Nor the gasping sob
Reaching deep into mucous caverns
And shuddering back again,
Sucking once more,
Throwing the tickling tear arcing silently
And more slide down the gleaming channel
Tremulous and hot
Heaving deep into the shaking body
Out into every pulsing vein
Till the raging wanes and there is
Only
A sweet aspen moaning.

Now just the taut cerebralisation of anguish
And a dry throat croak.

D. J. Kidd, 16

[170]

But no one cares

The day was long.
The winds blew on
But no one cared.

All alone,
Had no home,
But no one cared.

He fought against the wind and rain
Although he had a lot of pain,
But no one cared.

The day grew old
The night was cold
But no one cared.

The stars above
Were his only love
He left no mark
But no one cared.

He had feelings
Of his piteous meanings
But no one cared.

In the still of the night
He felt unright
But no one cared.

He could have died,
Instead he cried,
But no one cared.

[171]

Consciousness

The bumbling chatter liquefied and melted
Into one low hum, I sat, silent and foggy,
Remote in contemplation, hypnotised by thought,
As pain and fear, love and hate, and blank
Cold indifference travelled with me, escaping gradually
Through the dribbling windows. I thought:
'And there shall be Life—where stifled emotion
Preys on stifled imagination; then we shall all
Suffocate, and still our dumb minds with worldly thoughts,
And render our broiling consciences inactive,
And rid ourselves of depth and feeling,
And become remote as our thoughts.
Who am I? What am I? Where am I?
I am human. I am sensible. I am travelling on a bus.'

Nita Cameron

Breakfast

Cobwebs glisten like silver veils
  In the morning mist.
There is no noise save that of birds,
  As we walk down the quiet road.
Rounding the corner it hits you
  Like some unwieldy spaceship;
The great dining hall.
  I climb the steps like prisoner condemned;
But once inside I shut myself in
  From all people whom I hate,
And my thoughts go back to those
  Cobwebs glistening like silver veils
In the morning mist.
  A church bell far off strikes one,
And the air is filled with wondrous sounds:
  Waterfalls bounding down boulder strewn hills,
Autumn leaves blown up by wind,
  And I see,
Cobwebs glistening like silver veils,
  In the morning mist.
What stupidity it is that we have to eat,
What a waste of time each meal.
I eat everything which is placed before me,
  Not caring whence it comes or where it goes.
The bell strikes again
  And we are out once more,
Where cobwebs glisten like silver veils
  In the morning mist.

Simon Rycroft

Getting Home

Getting home after a weary day at school
I find it easier to write.

What used to be a hatred of mine
is now
one of my best hobbies.
Poetry,
I love writing poetry
It gives me a relaxed feeling
inside of myself . . .

Neil Hoggan, 13

[174]

It is so difficult to see the sun
With open eyes,
So difficult to dream about the moon
And feel its paleness,
So difficult to touch the softness
Of a lovely leaf,
Knowing the sadness of its
Solitude.
It is so very difficult to pray
And be content and sure
The echo of your cry
Will grow the hope and bring—perhaps—
The illusion
Of a simple happiness.

Maria Matsas (Greek)

[175]

Far-off in time, behind the hills,
Humble hands glorify the plough
In the stillness of the fields
Fulfil the earth with their vow.

Up, up high, to the bird's unreachable flight,
Down, down to the very bowels of the earth
Simple hands stretch and clutch, for the right
Of man to give, and get from the earth his birth.

A casual caress to a sleeping daisy taught my hands
How to possess the vastness of fairy-lands.

Simonetta de Paolis (Italian)

[176]

Tracks

Engraved on endless sand,
The microdot railway line
Of the weevil's arduous progress,
And the corkscrew of the adder,
Are harmless, under the sun.

But some patterns have
A deadly meaning. The flurried ground,
The urgent tracks, the piece of fur,
The drops of blood disturb
The methodical calm of the tracks
Under the sun.

Where are the tracks of human misery?
In every shaded glance, in downcast eyes,
In staring type, in tears. In the mind
And conscience you can see them
Lying naked and exposed
Under the sun.

David Gardiner

[177]

Stress of Life

O, the effort of being born,
Lungs expanding, first breath drawn.
O, the strain of trying to walk,
And the frustration of learning to talk.
O, the wonder of childhood eyes,
O, the torture of teenage whys?
Knowing the difference between right and wrong,
And the nightmares of the Hydrogen Bomb.
Rush, tear, noise and clamour,
Deadens all this so-called glamour.

O, the agony of first love spurned,
O, the joy of love returned.
O, the stress of family life,
Worry, work, toil and strife.
Then when all have left the fold.
What is left?
Despair of growing old.

Christopher Pinch

[178]

Spider Country

I have left there now and though
I never liked the place, I'm sorry.
When I was small I'd pick webs of dew
From the sharp yellow gorse, wary
Of lurking spiders on my way to school;
Crossing the ditch, always whispering secret water;
Shadows of trees were legs and the spider real.
In the pine-forest the spiders were smaller
But more numerous; a floor of fallen needles
Became a mortuary of insect limbs.
When one lodged in my crawling hair
I would run hard at the wind
Begging it to free the spider and my fear.

Where I am now is a different place
And I act as befits the change.
I wear my hair swept from my face
And though wind-struck is all the rage.
My home is comfortable, clean and free
of all insects: woodworm, moth and spider.
The roads are well-lit and lined by trees
Without branches, I feel, on the whole, safer.
Yet sometimes I long to go back
To the other place despite the fear,
But I'm told you never go back
Unless you are old and death is very near.

Jeremy Harris, 17

Pebbles

My life is like a pebble beach
A conglomeration of incidents:
Stranded as if by accident
Washed up upon the shore.

Pebbles:
Once a continent, born of a land.

Like pebbles—
Each moment clawed and dug out,
Carved from the cliff of time,
Shapeless at first, but rounded
As the sea begins to chime:
Manufactured stone memories
Give character to mind
Form a personality, made by others
Labelled mine.

Pick up a few pebbles
To make a picture in your hand
Look back from the long peninsula
At the beach down which you ran.
The bent and buckled body
Mirrors a lonely band
Of pebbles never lasting
Turning into sand
To be taken by the sea
As ashes of the land.

David Cann, 17

Scrap

In the breaker's yard the rusty metal stands,
Like huge silent sentinels of despair,
Waiting in forbidding mounds, high in the air,

The twisted piles, so menacing up there
Are the remnants of shining cars, and,
So many other things, too numerous to list.

Yet the tons of mighty metal are immortal;
They will start afresh with a second chance,
To be forged and cast unto the very last,
Remelted and machined to live again.
It goes like an unending chain.
Never will the immortal metal pass extinct.

Oh! if only we could start again,
When we become old and rusty.
There is no second chance, alas,
Perhaps if men were recast again,
They would become like solid metal,
Cold and hard, cast in the same iron mould.

Robert Paling

[181]

The End of the World

It will come very slowly
The Plants will grow very large
Creeping silently covering all the world.
Roots of trees will tear up buildings
Creeping plants will become six times as big
Silently covering buildings.

Janice Coulton, 12

Postscript

This collection is representative of the norm of poetry writing by young people; it is not a collection of prize pieces, though a few are included. It would not be difficult to produce a similar anthology every year, for of the thousands of schools in the country only about two hundred are represented here, and many an application for permission to print brought in more poems of quality. The schools include every type—infant, primary, grammar, comprehensive, modern, approved; schools for maladjusted children; independent schools, day and boarding, girls and boys; village colleges, technical colleges, centres for further education, and a college for foreigners learning English. A few items come from overseas and a few from the past, but most were written in England in recent years.

The anthology needs no apology, and thus the discussion that follows is placed at the end of the book. The poems stand on their merits as material for the general reader. They should interest teachers, too, and their pupils, who are always glad to read the work of their peers and will find encouragement to write themselves. Through the influence of Wordsworth and others, the years of immaturity are no longer regarded as a phase to be tolerated, but as an important stage with valid experiences. Thus the reading of hundreds of poems for this anthology never palled. Most of them had some interest—and where they had not the lack was sometimes due to adult influence—and many were most attractive, in their ever new and spirited response to the scenes and situations that prompted them. One could hardly be so buoyant after reading a similar quantity of adult verse.

Of the kinds of verse-writing by young people, one is fortunately less common than it was. Here it is, fifty years ago:

To a Celandine

In the dark and dreary nights
    When wild the winds do blow,
The little golden celandine
    Lies snug amid the snow.

This pretty little celandine
    In days so light and clear
Lives in the shade and lovely glade
    Which is so sweet and dear.

But when the days are fairer
And milder breezes blow
The little golden celandine
To Paradise shall go.

Child, 12 (1915)

And half a century later we still find poems of this kind:

Jack Frost

When Jack Frost wanders out at night
His magic fills me with delight.
The very first thing that I see,
Are little curtains made for me.

And in the garden I can tell,
That Jack's been working here as well.
The spiders' webs with pearls are strung,
And from the bushes neatly hung.

The garden is a lovely sight,
With all the hedges silver bright.
A-gay with tinsel in the sun,
To show how well his work is done.

The little fish pond as I pass,
Is now a shining piece of glass,
And on the roof-tops overhead,
There's sugar icing neatly spread.

In both, subjects which the child thinks will please adults have
been given the treatment thought appropriate, with sugary senti-
ment, jingling rhymes and conventional epithets. This was the
staple of children's poetry writing till about thirty years ago.
Compare both with a poem turned up at random—'The Pebble'
(No. 81)—where the writer is not only enjoying and learning the
manipulation of words and rhythm, but is also enjoying the pebble
more for having written about it.

Then teachers began to encourage a wider range of subject and

174

the use of free verse, and children began to produce a second type of writing. In the apprentice stage they wrote what were essentially prose accounts of experiences, rather mechanically cut up into lengths to look like verse. Teachers have never despised these efforts because they know that the writers at least learn to select their material and to concentrate on how to say it. Teachers again know that children can readily move on to writing poems the shape of which is decided by the need to communicate, where repetition and imagery are found, and where different lengths of line are used for movement or for emphasis, to increase the impact of a word or a phrase. The form comes from within. Examples of this development are Nos. 47, 27, 40, 63 and many others.

A third class includes poems by more sophisticated writers, who may be too conscious of their audience, or of the wrong kind of audience, and imitate styles and adopt stances that are in vogue. It can be dismissed as immature adult poetry, but it should more often be regarded as a stage of trying out modes that can lead on to something more personal.

The young poet is aware of a different audience from that at which the adult poet aims, for he is not concerned to flatter his readers as members of a group, to shock them or to show off in front of them. Instead he is writing for his peers and a few sympathetic adults, and consequently at his best he writes directly and as effectively as he can, without tiresome attitudinising and affectation. The adult poet on the other hand is more of a specialist. He has more poetic devices at his disposal to express the greater range of theme and response that should come with maturity, and more skill and experience in deploying them. He is a professional, with insights that can be communicated only in poetry. Young writers are not specialists, not capable of great range or penetration and not endowed with a highly developed technique—though many of them evince a skill that is fully adequate to their purpose. (Examples at random are Nos. 84 and 168.) And that is to produce and record the fresh response of a growing mind to situations and experiences that are new to it. Some of them reveal considerable poetic skill in conventional modes, but they are not necessarily very interesting; their work perhaps resembles the earlier attempts of those who later become established poets, attempts that (like the schoolboy verse of Matthew Arnold, for example) are exercises in the adult manner of the time by someone who has more desire to be a poet than matter of urgency to express.

Many children, perhaps most, can express themselves in verse, and readily; even the setting of a poem for homework can evoke something worth writing, because it offers the opportunity for a developing attitude to take shape and for unrealised feelings to find an articulate form. Later the writing capacity that is there is often stunted by an education that concentrates on the intellect, neglects the emotions and prescribes one limited mode of expression—the prose of report and statement and argument. Poetry is a way of response, a human faculty the atrophy of which means a serious loss. The inability to use the language of poetry precludes the experiences that can exist only through poetry, and blocks a way of being.

Given then the right conditions young writers will produce not imitation adult poetry but a personal response to the experiences they are likely to meet. (The confidence of that generalisation comes from the reading of much verse from many types of school.) 'The right conditions' mean in most cases a teacher who will provide stimulus and prompting and helpful interest. Naturally, as can be seen in these pages, the range of theme will be limited and predictable, nor shall we expect to find much in the way of wit or irony. This predictability may lead to misunderstanding. If a girl or boy writes a poem on spring it need not be because the teacher has imposed a dilute Wordsworthianism, but because the subject is natural and central to young people, and writing about it the evidence of a normal humanity. Very few will continue to write or read poetry after leaving school, because of a narrowing. As Raymond Williams has so well said, it is from such 'creative' activities that comes 'much of man's real society, and they should be given that kind of respect throughout education'. He continues

In the changes that come with puberty, it is vital that the practice of these activities should be continued, with no setting of 'more real' or 'more practical' work above them. Otherwise there is unnecessary fading, and all the major arts are relegated to the sphere of 'leisure': a separation which in itself makes inevitable, and much deeper than it ever now needs to be, a separation between art and society. Both sides then suffer: the arts because they are seen as marginal and specialized; society because it is limited to economics and administration. It is depressing to think that much of this division is now actively taught and learned in our schools, which at an earlier stage do so much to show how important and satisfying the arts can be to almost everyone.

Communications, p. 139

It is only in the last fifty years or so that children have been encouraged to write poetry. Before this century there were set pieces, special cases like that of Marjory Fleming (1803-1811), and the juvenilia of adult poets, but the writing of verse formed no part of the nineteenth-century picture of childhood nor of educational theory. It had no place for instance in P. J. Hartog's *The Writing of English* (1907), a book influential for some years, where the skills to be acquired are conceived in terms of the ability to write technical or military reports. (Incidentally it contains a splendid collection of topical-sounding complaints from employers about the poor English of school leavers.) But today teachers commonly encourage verse-writing to an extent evident in the number of recent books on the subject and in articles in the educational press. It has only recently been practised in other countries, such as South Africa and Australia—and here through the enterprise of a very few teachers; certainly the scale on which it flourishes in England is unparalleled. The next few pages will trace the rise of the phenomenon and consider the aims set out and the results claimed.

Most writers on the subject have published in the last twenty-five years, but earlier there were two teachers who did good work in isolation and without much following. The narrow utilitarianism which Hartog represented was gradually submerged by the tide of more liberal thinking in education that started with Matthew Arnold, and by new findings about the growth and learning of children. (In his last Report, of 1882, Arnold wrote as an H.M.I. about 'the aim of calling forth, by some means or other, in every pupil a sense of pleasurable activity and creation'.) Baden-Powell, Montessori and Dalcroze were among those who led Caldwell Cook to the theory and practice of teaching that he expounded in his *Play-Way* (1917), but also more briefly and convincingly in his five *Perse Playbooks* (1912-1915), scarce volumes for the loan of which I am grateful to Christopher Parry. In them Cook explained why he encouraged the writing of verse, and offered samples of his pupils' work, both as works of art and as school exercises. Shortly after Cook, E. A. Greening Lamborn wrote his *The Rudiments of Criticism* (1916), a short book that probably circulated more widely and for longer than the bulky *Play-Way*, which despite respectful inclusion in many book lists seems to have made little impact on teachers. Lamborn was headmaster of an Oxford elementary school, and like another cultivated and influential elementary school head, George Sampson, was much read by teachers in secondary schools. His book was about the teaching of poetry, almost took for granted the desirability of verse-writing in school, and contained a substantial anthology of short poems by his pupils. In 1921 George Sampson (*English for the English*, Cambridge University Press, 1971 edition) proposed verse-writing— and *vers libre* at that—as part of a school English course.

The 1937 edition of the Board of Education's *Handbook of Suggestions for Teachers* noted that 'In many schools the children are encouraged to make their own attempts at verse composition. It is clear that they find real pleasure in this method of expressing their experiences and that, by so doing, they have in addition increased their power of appreciating the poetry they study.' Similar reasons for poetry writing in schools were advanced by Norman Callan in his *Poetry in Practice* (1938): 'the emotional release, and the clearer understanding of the work of others.' Then just before the war of 1939 Norman Morris in *First Fruits* compiled the largest collection of children's prose and verse that had so far appeared in print; as such it was a landmark. The contents however were not of great interest, consisting mainly of pieces composed to fit the teacher's idea of child-writing.

The first teacher to make out what may be termed the modern theory of verse-writing in schools was James Reeves. Writing in 1941 (*English in Schools*, Vol. I, No. 8) he contended that every child must be taught as if he were going to be a creative writer, because the aim of education must be self-realisation, and as a means of self-realisation writing is unique. Of writing, verse is the best form, and it must be free verse, because the mechanical difficulties of metre and rhyme can be discouraging to the young writer. Much of the writing on children's poetry that has appeared subsequently (regularly in *The Use of English*, for example) has expanded and clarified this view. At about the same time as James Reeves, Marjorie Hourd did the teaching on which was based her *Education of the Poetic Spirit* (1949). In this pioneer work Miss Hourd brought to bear her knowledge of teaching, literature and psychology to clarify and establish the function of verse-writing by children in a setting of general educational theory; it was followed ten years later by *Coming Into Their Own* (1959), a work written in collaboration with Miss G. E. Cooper, which explored the classroom situation more thoroughly and included a large amount of children's poetry. After them came Boris Ford's *Young Writers, Young Readers* (1960), *And When You Are Young*, collected by the London Association for the Teaching of English (1960),

David Holbrook's *English for Maturity* (1961), Sir Alec Clegg's remarkable *The Excitement of Writing* (1964, after previous local circulation), and many other books and articles; so that now hardly a year passes without the appearance of a book on verse-writing in school, and a mass-circulation daily runs an annual competition for children's writing, with the winning (and very cerebral) entries printed in book form. In addition schools, teachers' organisations and education authorities are constantly putting out collections, many of them engaging and of good quality.

To read the discussions of children's writing that have appeared in the last ten years is to accumulate the evidence for applying 'pioneer' to Miss Hourd's work. They echo again and again the words we find in her first book:

> In his growth from birth to maturity a person has to ask himself three important questions which correspond in a broad sense to the three chief stages of development. First he asks in early childhood: 'Who am I?' and he makes the assertion in as many ways as possible: 'I am myself.' Then he explores more fully his relationship to other people and through sympathy as well as rivalry reaches a degree of reciprocity. This is his main task in later childhood. Thirdly he explores further his own uniqueness and asks: 'What kind of a person am I?' This is the question of adolescence.

And then she goes on to illustrate the part played by children's writing in helping this growth. In all subsequent discussions of the purpose of encouraging children to write 'growth' is the key word. Boris Ford, for example, in the Introduction to his book writes 'this verse and prose represents an important and legitimate part of the business of growing up' and at about the same time the editors of *And When You Are Young* state their belief that 'children grow in personality by the simple process of talking or writing about what matters to them to someone who matters to them'. Finally, James Britton concludes an excellent article in Professor Ford's book with the words:

> Children, knowing comparatively little, are active explorers, using all their powers of imagination and intuition. When language assists in such exploration, what the children write will often be poetry. It will be poetry by virtue of its power to alter, in a certain way, the children's 'accumulated feelings about themselves'; and this despite any reader who in his adult wisdom and mature taste may find it 'paltry, trite and pointless'.

179

Children who write poetry are thereby in a better position to express their thoughts and feelings, and thus to clarify them and establish 'who they are'. This sense of identity is important, for according to Liam Hudson in *Frames of Mind* it exerts a controlling influence 'over the intellectual choices we make, and the mental abilities we are willing to reveal'. Caldwell Cook was thus ahead of his time when he wrote (in terms that would have been different had he lived thirty years later):

> The open secret of all this work is personality. It is the working-out of the personality of each boy in relation to other persons and things (including his teacher), and the interaction of character, that form the conditions in which this work is born.

After the affirmation and closer understanding of self the next stage is a firmer apprehension of reality. Again Caldwell Cook, though his pupils' work really gave him nothing to go on, pointed to the direction by which this closer grasp is attained: 'in the full realisation of a single issue, in the single representation of a deed or a thing seen, the average child is far superior to the average adult.' The child-poetry that Cook printed rarely gives even a hint of matching his account; characterless exercises for the most part in the poetic modes thought appropriate sixty years ago, they never 'realise' anything or convey any impression that the child has seen aught but the teacher's expectations.* This was clear to Cook: 'In the book as a whole the school atmosphere may be distinctly felt. In the preponderance of "nature" poems and of works fashioned closely on well-known models one can see that the master and what he is presumed to like are prominent in the minds of the boys.'

Even in Miss Hourd's *Coming Into Their Own* the children's poems do not always support the author's insights—which could certainly be confirmed by much of the work by young writers that has been published since her book appeared. There are now constantly being produced poems in which for example the writer's

---

* How very influential are these expectations can be seen in the San Francisco experiment recorded in ETC: *A Review of General Semantics*, Vol. 24, No. 4. Teachers but not pupils or parents were told falsely after an IQ test that a fifth of their pupils, named in a list over the whole ability range, would improve dramatically over a year. 'Almost as if by magic, each of these pupils listed made the predicted dramatic gains, while the rest of the student body did not . . . a year later the "spurters" showed an average gain of 12·2 points . . . many children turn out to be dull because their teachers expect them to be dull.'

sense of personal identity can be seen to develop and strengthen, or in which the child can be seen working out a primitive morality, when the exploration of ambivalence brings out the jar between opposite feelings. When a child is writing with his peers and/or teacher as audience there may be some support for Caldwell Cook's 'far superior', though at the stage of young adulthood the writers are liable to be conscious of a different readership and will be liable to write for effect accordingly. The 'superiority' will be more nearly attained if the teacher looks for 'evidence of strong feeling, interest, and involvement; sincerity and lack of affectation; a "right" selection of details; and a complete self-forgetfulness in the face of the absorbing task of recording an experience faithfully' (J. H. Walsh—on children's prose—p. 42, *Teaching English*). The freshness of response that can characterise children's poetry is valuable; developed and habitual it will help to prevent stock responses and stereotyped thinking and make for an openness to experience.

The case for encouraging a child to write poetry rests on three propositions. It helps him to establish his identity. This is a new or more urgent need, not always clear to older people, at a time when so many props and reassuring bounds as well as hampering restraints have been removed; according to Jack Beckett (in his *The Keen Edge*) the mass denial of identity that goes on in the factory actually starts at school. It helps him to know himself better, again especially important when so many versions of ourselves are busily offered by advertising and other agencies. (Another aspect is discussed by Liam Hudson on p. 86 of *Frames of Mind*.) It helps him by exploring experiences and relationships and 'digesting' them to arrive at a more adequate sense of reality. (Cf. David Holbrook: 'Creativity is a matter of relationship with oneself, that enables one to come to better terms with the outer world'— *Children's Writing*.)

Another aim is less heard of nowadays: the readier contact with literature afforded by writing poetry, claimed by Cook and Lamborn and by the Board of Education's 1937 *Suggestions*. Less heard of perhaps because the reading of literature is less in favour with some of those who write about teaching, possibly because they conceive it only as they have experienced it, as something examinable, specialised and academic, or merely as an expression of 'middle class culture'. David Holbrook on the other hand sees literature in this field of creative work as essential to the teacher— 'He can learn only by studying literature itself' to 'foster the kinds of sincerity and genuineness he knows to be in great art'; and essential to the child, who can be led to discover how others have met the problems that face him, and to connect the civilisation which is growing in him with the 'inheritance of civilisation on the shelves'.

When those with experience of verse-writing in school come to record the gains made, they rely on a basic view of poetry as a means of communicating what could not otherwise be expressed or indeed experienced: 'where poetry is not admissible, the experience will rarely be expressed at all, for there will be no inducement for most children to learn the difficult language of the poet. Lacking expression, the experience . . . will tend to lack meaning even for the child who had it' (James Britton). In *The Eye of Innocence* Robert Druce speaks for many teachers when he notes a 'deepening personal awareness' as one of the profits of verse-writing. Miss Hourd, always clear that the teacher's task is not that of the psychologist, records that she was 'struck over and over again by the help that verse writing brings to . . . children who suffer from psychic scars'. In observing that education through art 'by strengthening a sense of personal identity necessarily makes it easier for the individual to find his most useful place in society' Miss Hourd is followed by David Holbrook, who believes (*Universities Quarterly*, September 1967) that unless education helps to foster this sense of identity 'it will not be effective—not even effective in preparing individuals for practical matters in the world'.

When we come to consider methods of encouraging the writing of verse in school we find them many and varied, as a glance at back numbers of *The Use of English* will show. Miss Hourd describes the most important factor of all, the teacher's attitude:

> If then the teacher is the authority who makes it safe to say what you really want to say, and not the authority who dictates what it is you ought to say, it follows that the way the expression is received by the teachers becomes yet another aspect of the relation in education. A child does not feel free to express himself unless he feels that his expression will be protected. On the other hand, there comes a point when correction and instruction are necessary parts of this very safeguard. For a child not only wants to say what he means; he wants to say it well . . .

There must be trust between the teacher and the child writer; it may be that lack of the right kind of trust has till fairly recently precluded the readiness of children to write. The teacher will try to make the conditions right so that his pupils will feel free to write for him. For some children it will merely be a matter of 'leaving the way open'; for others experience in life and literature will have to be offered, for a start. Here the following have been found helpful: Anglo-Saxon poems, the ballads, Whitman, Lawrence, Pound, Carl Sandburg, Arthur Waley, Edgar Lee Masters and a number of modern poets. This book also has been planned to be of use in giving this start. From younger children the teacher will receive the poem (in Miss Hourd's words again) 'as one would receive a gift'. Adolescent writers will need to feel that their teacher cares and understands. The latter will not overdo the sympathising with a particular poem, but will express assent, recognition or approval, and perhaps—keeping the temperature reasonable—make suggestions or comment on a technical point.

Technique used to be taught first; both Cook and Lamborn went in for this. The position has now been abandoned, and the general view is nearer the other extreme: that given the need to say something in poetry children will usually find the mode of expression they want. It is unlikely that this will involve the use of rhyme, which may help practised writers but for most can be disastrous, inhibiting a fresh response and inducing a mere matching-up with the expectations that seem to go with rhyme. I have seen a school's whole output of poetry in its literary magazine vitiated and rendered trivial or dishonest by the unskilled resort to rhyme, probably in conformity with teacher-ideas. The latter may be necessary at the outset, when the child's notion of the poetic may need widening, but in the end good teaching will come out not in the adoption of a particular style but in the range and quality of pupils' poems. There are differing opinions about revision and fair copies, but most teachers seems to believe that some tidying up and polishing are needed before 'publication'. It need hardly be added that the writer's agreement should be obtained for this, and that the term includes reading aloud, circulation in the class and putting up on the board as well as printing or duplicating.

Before the time of James Reeves and Miss Hourd there seems to have been little verse-writing in school, except that appearing in school magazines, some of which was very good. The work produced for Caldwell Cook and Greening Lamborn is devoid of intrinsic interest today; it so often takes the form of impersonal exercises which do not engage the writer much more than the turning out of Greek and Latin verses at classical schools. In fact, in Lamborn's collection one finds the same couplet used by several writers, and with only slight variation by others. After Miss Hourd one sees the extension of poetry writing to different ages and different types of school; she was the first to point out that adequate verbal expression is not limited to those of good intelligence and that there remains 'for the person of average or lower intelligence a very rich field of expressiveness'. A good deal of the poetry written in schools nowadays is of a kind to engage and sustain the interest of an adult reader; and it amply supports the claims made by Miss Hourd, David Holbrook and James Britton.

Self-consciousness and consciousness of the adult world are now thrust upon children, whether we like it or not; the more 'civilised' a country is, the less are its children allowed to be children, as in 'normal' times they are happy and content to be. The writing of poetry seems to be a sphere in which children can be most truly themselves and can most healthily grow up; it should be nourished at school, whether or not children will read or write at all when they have left. It is a matter of arranging things so that they are allowed to use the resources described by Professor M. A. K. Halliday, quoted by Connie Rosen in *Primary English*, when he writes of the 'resources that we acquire so young':

> Anyone who learns to listen linguistically . . . can only be amazed at what children, and still more adults, can do with their native language . . . in this light we can perhaps get some idea of the wealth of imagination and resource with which the language is adapted by its speakers . . .

I believe that the collection illustrates the truth of what Professor Halliday says. Approaching the subject rather as an outsider, I have been convinced that those who see a means of growth in the writing of poetry of young people are fully justified, and that the process produces results which deserve our attention.

184

Index of First Lines

The numbers of the poems are given

Answer to riddle (poem no. 96): wheel.

Acknowledgments

The collection from which this anthology has been chosen has been accumulated over many years, largely by contributions from teachers, and without thought of publication. The idea of the book came from the publisher, on my observing that for use in teaching I had been reading hundreds of poems from schools, without flagging or loss of interest. However the way in which the poems have been gathered means that in a number of cases source and authorship have not been recorded, and even when there is a record changes of address have baffled repeated attempts to obtain permission. Consequently it has not been possible to secure consent for the inclusion of some of the poems in these pages, and for this I apologise. Any corrections or additions will be made in the next edition.

To Raymond O'Malley, who lent me his own collection; to the teachers who supplied many of the poems and gave much generous help; and to the schools, authorities and publishers who kindly gave permission to print the poems of which the numbers are given below, I am most grateful. Lastly I am glad to acknowledge my debt to the hundreds of writers whose poems have made the preparing of the anthology an enjoyable though not always easy task.

The numbers given are those of the poems.

Anthony Adams, *Inky Blots* (Churchfields School, West Bromwich): 2, 34
John Adams, *Quays and Crossroads* (Sevenoaks School): 66
A. E. Aston and Dennis Brook, *Abstract* (Alleyn's School, S.E. 22): 63
A. Bessell, *Poetry, Eleven to Eighteen* (S. W. Lancs Branch of the National Association for the Teaching of English): 14, 41, 142, 167, 181
Murray Biggs, *Wolf* (Eton College): 73, 124, 133
C. P. Birnie, *The Stortfordian*: 125; and *New Wine* (both Bishop's Stortford College): 169, 179, 91, 92, 114, 122, 173
Mrs Penny Blackie, W. Suffolk Association for Teaching English, *And This is Happiness*: 1, 27, 116
Patrick Brady, *Themes 1962* (Charlton Boys' School): 180
J. F. W. Brown and the Editors, *At First Sight* (Poems and Prose from Brighton Schools): 164
John Charlesworth (Spalding Grammar School): 59, 71, 126, 127, 141, 152
Chatto and Windus Ltd. and the Editor, *The Use of English*: 12, 22, 29, 42, 68, 69, 96, 99, 107, 108, 118, 135, 137, 151, 168, 171

Through English (Oxford University Press): 84; *Primary English*: 64, 161

The Rev. J. P. Newell, Headmaster, The King's School, Canterbury: 65

The Headmistress, North London Collegiate School, *Janus*: 158

W. P. Payne, *The Burnt Mill*: 13, 18, 52, 119, 178; and *Winter Warmers* (both Burnt Mill Comprehensive School, Harlow): 17

Andrew Pierce, *Clifton College Writing*, Spring 1969: 23, 177

Anthony J. Pike, *The Ecclesfieldian* (The Grammar School, Ecclesfield, nr. Sheffield): 104, 110, 128, 159

David Schonveld, *Collection of Poems by the Poetry Group of 2A* (Braehead School, Buckhaven, Fife): 138, 174

G. V. Stamford, Librarian, Bedales School Memorial Library, *Bedales Chronicle*: 120

J. M. Stratford (Kimbolton School, Huntingdonshire): 16 (published in *Pen to Paper*, Cambridge Institute of Education)

Elfed Thomas, Director of Education, City of Leicester Education Department, Children's Writing: 9, 43, 86, 88, 157, 170

Richard Tucker, *The Ipswichian* (Ipswich School, Suffolk): 95, 90

J. H. Walsh, R. A. Cole and F. Tomlinson, *The Chronicle* (Chislehurst and Sidcup Grammar School for Boys): 24, 40, 53, 85

Peter Watson (formerly of Leeds Modern School): 75, 144

Sir Alec Clegg, The County Council of the West Riding of Yorkshire, and Chatto and Windus, Ltd. *The Excitement of Writing*: 39, 89, 130, 140, 162

The illustrations are reproduced from the *Sunday Mirror* National Exhibition of Children's Art 1970 by kind permission of the *Sunday Mirror* and the following artists:

Maria Fernandez, Chester School of Art: 4

Pamela Riches, Tollesbury County Primary School, Maldon: 8

Karen Clement, Timorfa Infants School, Port Talbot: 15

Sylvia Loveitt, Turves Green Secondary Girls' School, Northfield, Birmingham: 30

Barbara Elliott, Queen Anne's School, Caversham: 38

Lesley Marrion, Abraham Darby Comprehensive School, Madeley: 50–1

Rosemary Slade, The Green School for Girls, Isleworth: 59

Janet Dunkley, Dunhurst (Bedales Junior School), Petersfield: 64

Kerry Wood, Shears Green Junior School, Northfleet, Gravesend: 77

Graham Jenkin, Helston County Secondary School: 95

Matthew Willcox, Brookside House School, Harrow Weald: 108

Shona McVicar, Rashfield School, Dunoon, Argyll: 111

Sheridan Morley, St. Ann's Heath County Primary School: 122

Benjamin Holgate, Lancaster: 130

Winhills Junior School, St. Neots (Group Work): 136

Ann Thornley, School of Arts and Crafts, Burton-on-Trent: 146

Deborah Carr, Abbey Park Infants' School, Pershore: 162.